chloë owens

all sewn up

35 exquisite projects using appliqué, embroidery, and more

CICO BOOKS

LONDON NEW YORK

Textile artist Chloë Owens inhabits a strange and colorful world where fabric animals frolic, sequinned birds sing, and even the landscape is made up of groovy 1960s prints. In the heart of London she has sewn her own enchanted wilderness, turning her hand to greetings cards, a menagerie of soft toys, bespoke canvasses, and comfy cushions. Chloë hoards salvaged vintage fabrics and combines them with contemporary prints to create a totally new fabric that she "draws" delicate stitched designs on to using her trusty sewing machine. The result is a multifaceted textile feast! All her pieces are bespoke originals and she is available for commissions for all your crafting needs. Visit her website at www.chloeowens.com

This book is dedicated to the adoring memory of Jake, my cheeky and sweet-natured special friend who passed away during the making of this book. He made me smile and filled my days with sunshine.

This paperback edition published in 2018 by CICO Books
An imprint of Ryland Peters & Small Ltd

20–21 Jockey's Fields
London WC1R 4BW

341 E 116th St
New York, NY 10029

www.rylandpeters.com

10 9 8 7 6 5 4 3 2 1

First published in 2012

A CIP catalog record for this book is available from the Library of Congress and the British Library.

ISBN: 978 1 78249 672 4

Printed in China

Editor: Kate Haxell
Designer: Christian Owens
Illustrator: Gemma Correll
Photographer: Claire Richardson
Additional photography on pages 13, 19, 32, 33, 35 top and middle, 48–49, 66–78, 96–98, 104–107, 110, 112–113: Gavin Kingcome
Cut-out photography: Martin Norris

Hello!

My name is Chloë Owens, I'm a textile designer and illustrator, and I enjoy nothing more than collecting vibrant vintage fabrics and recycling them to make beautiful things.

Likes/dislikes: I like tea and biscuits and my favorite band is the Beatles. I love animals and am a vegetarian who craves meat. I love comedy and friends who can make me laugh. I don't like queues, being cold, or when people squash spiders.

I'm in love with color and pattern and completely obsessed by the 1960s—a time when I think the vibrancy of color, pattern, and playfulness was at its peak. Sadly I missed that era by a couple of decades, so I just have to recreate it in my own way, by collecting 1960s bed sheets, curtains, and anything else I can get my hands on from markets and rummage sales: it's so satisfying to pop into a goodwill shop and find a genuine hidden gem. Even just by rummaging through my mom's wardrobe I've found some amazing old unused pillowcases and snazzy '60s–70s dresses that have ended up being recycled into a doll's dress, a toy bunny (see page 42), or a new cushion (such as the swirly, twirly pom-pom pillow on page 104).

My most-loved method of working is with fabric appliqué, putting together bits cut out from a 1960s pillowcase with a flower from an old Scandinavian table cloth, and combining these with swirling psychedelic Liberty lawns and fancy stitching. Breathing life into neglected fabrics by mixing them together to make something completely new is wonderfully satisfying.

I always loved art and was constantly drawing, but never really thought I was any good at it. Then one day I discovered I was quite nifty on a sewing machine! I didn't like using it in the conventional way; instead, I used an embroidery presser foot to "draw" with stitch, and I cut up bits of fabric to "color in" my pictures. This way of working came much more naturally to me than drawing with pencils and paints. I began to learn that the more fluidly I worked, and the less I worried about mistakes, the better the design would look in the end. Even if there were tangled threads and wiggly lines, the finished piece had an undeniable charm and offered me a freedom I couldn't find with other mediums.

I work in a sunny spare room-come-studio at home and I'm kept company by my cat, Jake, who has smiley eyes and who likes to get involved in everything I do. Jake likes chewing plastic bags, chasing Barney, my sister's dog, and waking me up in the night by tapping me on the nose. He dislikes the vacuum cleaner, having his feet touched and being woken up. He loves to knock my buttons and beads onto the floor with his paws, run away with cotton reels, get tangled up in my threads, and bury himself in piles of my fabrics so I have to wash them all over again. Another thing he's discovered as a fun pastime is to dip his paws in my tea. Anyway, you'll be meeting more of him throughout this book.

I'm inspired by everything around me: if you look hard enough, you can find patterns in anything. A bathroom tile, a garden trellis, a bedroom rug: have a look and you'll begin to notice pattern everywhere. Once you're in this mode, ideas will come to you and you'll discover the ability to express them through your creations. Sometimes the ideas will work and sometimes they won't—but it's always fun trying them out. Music also inspires me; I love listening to '60s music while I work on a colourful canvas with clashing colors and patterns. I also have a thing for birds in my designs, as you might begin to notice throughout this book. Think about what you love and incorporate it in to your designs—then you'll really come into your own and find your true potential. If you have a passion for what you're making, others will, too.

What I'd most like you to take from this book is the encouragement to have fun in what you do. Clash your prints, be creative with color, doodle with your sewing machine, let your creativity run away with you! Discover your own style through new ways of working and thinking about textiles. If you take a shine to sequins and you're barmy about buttons and beads, incorporate them into a design; if you like padding out shapes, you can use batting (wadding) and layers of fabrics to create a 3-D effect. Instead of buying pillows (cushions) for your sofa, why not make your own? Or rather than spending money on an expensive toy, why not hand-make a personalized version, such as George the Giraffe on page 44? And rather than buy a present for a friend's birthday, make one that's unique. It's so rewarding, and I guarantee they'll appreciate it and treasure it much more. Don't be afraid of things not turning out perfectly—or exactly how you imagined—because that will happen from time to time. The results aren't a "mistake": they are a perfect opportunity for learning, and you may love the "mistake" more than the original design. That's the way my style has developed into what it is today, and the only way you'll develop and grow as a designer and maker yourself.

I hope this book inspires you and makes you smile.

Chloë Owens
&
Jake

Cooking up a storm

Keep clean and stay cool apron

I'm infatuated with aprons, which is funny because I rarely cook! There's just something about them that is so appealing, and they don't have to be cutesy. This is a great project for recycling old fabrics, and the result is perfect for looking stylish at summer barbecues.

Crafty needs!

Templates on page 134

Fading fabric marker

Blue felt

Scraps of fabric for appliqué details

Fabric glue

1 piece of plain fabric measuring 24 x 16¹/₂in (60 x 42cm)

Pins, needles, and scissors

Sewing machine with embroidery foot

Sewing threads in colors of your choice

3yd (3m) of bias tape, bought or made

1 piece of patterned fabric measuring 24 x 7¹/₂in (60 x 19cm) and 1 piece measuring 20¹/₄ x 4in (51 x 10cm)

Iron

Tape measure

Ribbon for the ties

1 Enlarge the templates by 200 percent and use the fabric marker to draw two whole birds onto the felt (see page 128), flipping the template over so they face each other. Cut the back and tummy pieces from scraps of fabric and use a small amount of fabric glue to stick them in place (see page 128). Cut the birds out and position them so that they're facing each other on the front of the plain fabric, at least 9in (23cm) up from the bottom and 4in (10cm) down from the top. Use fabric glue or pins to hold the motifs in place, and then free-machine embroider (see page 130) around each bird. Add different colored threads to define the wings.

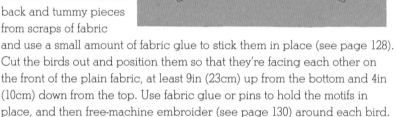

2 Cover the top raw edge of the pocket (the larger piece of patterned fabric) with bias tape. Cut a 24-in (60-cm) length of tape and press it in half lengthwise. Slip the top edge of the fabric into the fold and pin it in place, making sure there are no puckers. Machine sew (see page 128) a straight or decorative stitch along the lower edge of the tape, stitching through all layers.

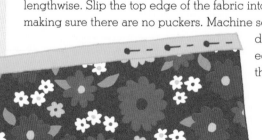

3 Pin the pocket to the lower part of the appliquéd fabric, aligning the bottom and side edges. Measure the width and, using the fading marker, mark two evenly spaced vertical lines on the pocket fabric. Using a decorative machine stitch, sew along the lines to make three separate pockets.

4 To gather the top of the apron, set the sewing machine to the longest straight stitch, or hand sew a loose running stitch along the edge, about ¼in (5mm) down from the top. Leave enough thread at either end to pull up the gathers. Now pull each end of the thread slowly and carefully to create even gathers without breaking the thread. Stop when the top of the apron measures about 20in (50cm).

Nearly there!
Now add a nice ribbon
(once I've untangled Jake).

5 Now add ribbon ties. Measure the ribbon around your waist to get an idea of the length needed: it's better too long than too short, because you can always trim it. To make sure the ties will be equal lengths, fold the ribbon in half and cut it into two. Position a piece on either side of the back of the apron, with one end against a top corner as shown, and backstitch (see page 132) in place.

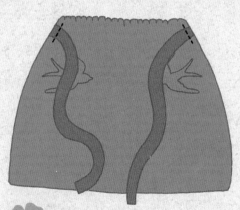

6 Fold under and press a ¼-in (5-mm) hem along the long edges of the remaining piece of patterned fabric. Choose a thread that blends well with the fabric and machine sew the hems. Then fold the fabric in half so the long hemmed edges meet, and press the fold. Slip the gathered top of the apron into the fold and pin it in place to make a waistband; trim off any excess fabric at each end. Machine sew a straight or decorative stitch along the lower edge of the waistband, stitching through all layers.

7 Press the rest of the bias tape in half. Fold under and press one short end to neaten it. Beginning at the top of one side, pin the tape over the raw edges, including the ends of the ribbon ties. Pin it in place all around the apron, trimming the tape and folding under the other end when you get there. Carefully machine sew the bias tape in place, smoothing out any puckers as you go.

Tantalizing tea towel

Tea towels are the perfect way to express your creativity; just make each one an artwork you can use to dry the dishes!

1 If you are making a tea towel, press under a double 1-in (2.5-cm) hem on the long edges and then the short edges. Pin the hems in place. Set the sewing machine to a medium straight stitch (see page 128) and sew each hem. You're done!

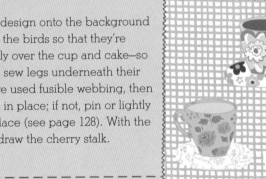

2 There are a million different designs you could sew: for my tea and cake design I've used 12 different fabrics, but you can use as many or as few as you like. Enlarge the templates by 200 percent and cut out all the pieces from fabrics and felts (see page 128). (If you are using fusible webbing, see page 128 for tips.) For the birds you'll need felt for the bodies and different fabrics for the wings and breasts. Choose a patterned fabric for the background: I've chosen a blue and white check fabric measuring 12 x 16½in (30 x 41cm), and I cut it with pinking shears for a decorative edge and to stop it fraying.

3 Collage the design onto the background fabric; position the birds so that they're hovering slightly over the cup and cake—so there's room to sew legs underneath their bodies. If you've used fusible webbing, then iron the pieces in place; if not, pin or lightly glue them in place (see page 128). With the fabric marker, draw the cherry stalk.

4 Take the design to the sewing machine and, using coordinating threads, free-machine embroider (see page 130) the elements. If you're feeling confident, try out different embroidery stitches to add more interest. Sew around the birds in a few different colors—no need to be neat here, just try to work with a fluid motion. And remember to sew them some legs! Add detail to the bottom of the cupcake and use colored threads to hand-embroider sprinkles on the frosting using straight stitches (see page 132).

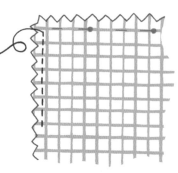

Now drying the dishes won't feel like such a chore!

5 Pin the background fabric in position on the tea towel. With the feed dogs down, set the sewing machine to a medium straight stitch and sew around the edges, about ½in (1cm) in from the pinked edges.

The fly-away-umbrella tea cozy

I like tea, especially tea with biscuits. When you have a pile of work waiting for you, or you've had a bad day, there's nothing better than a nice cuppa to put things to rights: it's like magic. To make the tea-time experience even more pleasant, just add this very sophisticated tea cozy.

Crafty needs!

Teapot!
Tape measure
Paper
Pins, needles, and scissors
Fabric for tea cozy
Batting (wadding)
Felt for lining
Fusible interfacing
Iron
Scraps of fabric for appliqué design
Templates on page 135
Fading fabric marker
Sewing machine with embroidery foot
Fabric glue (optional)
Sewing threads in colors of your choice
Ribbon for handle loop

1 First you will need to measure the height and circumference of your teapot and, from paper, cut out a cozy-shaped pattern piece that will fit it. Add a ½-in (1-cm) seam allowance all the way around. Then use this pattern to cut out two pieces from the main fabric, two from the batting (wadding), two from the lining felt, and one from interfacing. Iron the interfacing to the back of one piece of the main fabric: this will be the front of the cozy.

2 Enlarge the templates by 200 percent (or as needed to fit your cozy) and cut out the hair, face, hands, coat, skirt, legs, socks, shoes, and umbrella from different fabrics (see page 128). Collage the pieces onto the front of the cozy. Remember, it doesn't have to look completely neat, but try to think about the space and play around with the design until you're happy with it. Glue or pin the pieces in place (see page 128).

3 Using threads of your choice (I used lighter colors for the highlights and black for most of the outlines), free-machine embroider (see page 130) around the picture, adding detail to the pockets, skirt and coat ruffles, hair, and face. Embroider the umbrella handle. Feel free to add more detail if you want, such as birds, butterflies, or even raindrops made with sequins or beads.

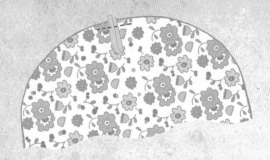

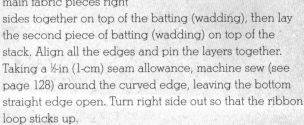

4 Fold a strip of ribbon in half and press it. Baste (tack) it to the top of the right side of the undecorated piece of main fabric, with the looped end facing down.

5 Lay one batting (wadding) piece flat, place the two main fabric pieces right sides together on top of the batting (wadding), then lay the second piece of batting (wadding) on top of the stack. Align all the edges and pin the layers together. Taking a ½-in (1-cm) seam allowance, machine sew (see page 128) around the curved edge, leaving the bottom straight edge open. Turn right side out so that the ribbon loop sticks up.

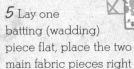

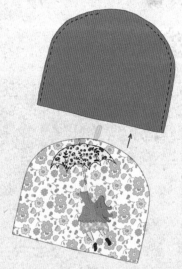

6 Pin the lining pieces right sides together and sew around the curved edge as in Step 5, but leaving a 4-in (10-cm) opening at the center top. Leave this piece wrong side out.

7 Push the main fabric and wadding piece into the lining piece, so that the right side of the main fabric is facing the right side of the lining. Match and pin the bottom edges. Stitch around the bottom edge, taking a ½-in (1-cm) seam allowance.

8 Carefully pull the cozy right side out through the hole in the top of the lining. Pull the main fabric right through, then keep pulling until the lining is turned completely right side out. Slip stitch (see page 132) the gap in the lining closed. Push the lining inside the cozy, give the whole thing a quick iron to smooth out any creases, and you've done it!

Time for tea!

Pretty-pleasing-sugar-on-top placemats

Brighten up dinnertime and impress your guests with these Scandinavian-inspired placemats.

1 Choose a background fabric: you will need two pieces measuring 15 x 15in (37 x 37cm) for each placemat. Then choose a selection of colored felts that complement the background fabric.

2 Iron fusible interfacing (see page 128) onto the wrong side of the front fabric. With the fabric marker and ruler, draw a line down the center. Enlarge the template by 300 percent and place the dotted line on the drawn line. Draw the swirls and leaves (see page 128), then flip the template and draw them on the other side of the line. Using a decorative machine stitch, sew the center line. Then lower the feed dogs and free-machine embroider (see page 130) the swirls and leaves.

3 Cut out all the birds, hearts, and flowers from felt and glue or pin them (see page 128) symmetrically on the fabric. Using coordinating threads and straight stitch, free-machine embroider around each element.

Crafty needs!

Fabrics and felts

Fusible interfacing

Iron

Fading fabric marker

Ruler

Pins, needles, and scissors

Template on page 136

Sewing machine with embroidery foot

Sewing threads to tone with fabrics and felts

Fabric glue (optional)

Heat-proof batting (wadding)

Invite friends around for dinner and flaunt your fabulous mats.

4 Cut a piece of batting 14.5 x 14.5in (36 x 36cm). Put the two pieces of fabric right sides together and lay the batting on top. Pin, then sew around the edges, taking a ½-in (1-cm) seam allowance and leaving a 5-in (13-cm) gap. Trim the corners (see page 130). Turn right side out and press, pressing under the seam allowances across the gap. Topstitch (see page 129) around the mat with a contrast thread.

Woodland critters table runner

Decorate your table with style with this intricately elaborate woodland critters table runner.

1 Cut the main fabric to size: mine is 50 x 15in (125 x 37cm). From purple felt, cut hill shapes to fit along both long edges, using the photo as a guide to shape. Pin or glue the hills in place (see page 128). Using a medium straight stitch, machine-sew (see page 128) along the edges of the hills in matching thread. Next, draw freehand swirls on the hills with the fabric marker. Lower the feed dogs and free-machine embroider (see page 130) over the lines with contrast thread.

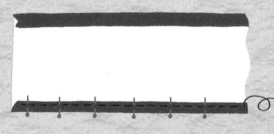

2 Fold under and pin a double ½-in (1-cm) hem along both long edges. Using a medium straight stitch, machine sew the hems. Do the same for the short ends.

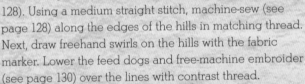

3 Enlarge the templates by 200 percent and cut out trees and animals from your chosen fabrics and felts. (If you are using fusible webbing, see page 128 for tips.) I cut pairs of trees and animals, but you don't have to make your design regular in the same way.

Let the table runner take center stage at dinner time.

4 Lay the runner flat and, working from one end to the other, arrange half the trees and animals along one side and pin, glue, or iron them in place (see page 128). Flip the fabric so that the trees and animals you've just positioned are upside down, and arrange the remaining pieces in the same order, working from the opposite direction. Pin or glue these in place, too.

5 With threads of your choice, free-machine embroider around each tree and animal, adding details to the deer's face and speckles on its back, and sewing the squirrel's whiskers. Sometimes I use a sketchy "drawing" technique, but for this project I've gone round the fabric edges neatly, and just once. Trim any unruly threads.

Hop, skip, and a pair of oven mitts

We can't all be a kitchen goddess, but we can at least pretend with these divine and dandy oven mitts. They're quick and easy to make, perfect for presents, and they jazz up the kitchen a treat.

1 Enlarge the apple template by 200 percent. Draw the main apple shape twice onto the webbing and cut around about ½in (1cm) outside the lines (see page 128). Iron the webbing onto the apple fabric (see page 128), then cut out two apples. Cut out the rest of the apple pieces twice from felts.

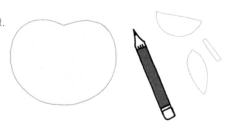

2 Enlarge the small mitt template by 400 percent and cut two from the mitt pieces of fabric. Position a brown stalk on a mitt and iron an apple to the center of the mitt, overlapping the end of the stalk. Layer the other felt pieces on top—the red half, the white core, and the brown seeds. Then add the leaves. Pin or glue the pieces in place (see page 128). Repeat with the second small mitt piece.

3 Using free-machine embroidery (see page 130), sew around all the elements of the apple design with coordinating threads.

Crafty needs!

Templates on page 136

Fusible webbing

Pins, needles, and scissors

Iron

5 different fabrics and felts for the apple

Fading fabric marker

2 pieces of mitt fabric measuring 9 x 8½in (23 x 21.5cm)

Fabric glue (optional)

Sewing machine with embroidery foot

Sewing threads to tone with fabrics and felts

2 pieces of main fabric and 1 piece of heat-proof batting (wadding) measuring 33 x 9in (84 x 23cm)

Approx 2½yd (2.5m) of bias binding

4 Cut two lengths of bias binding to fit across the straight edge of the small mitt pieces: it's best to cut them a bit longer and trim them later. Press the bias binding in half lengthwise and slip the straight edge of each mitt piece into the fold. Pin the binding in place. With the feed dogs up, set the sewing machine to a medium straight stitch (see page 128) and sew the binding to the mitt, removing pins as you go.

5 Enlarge the long mitt piece by 400 percent. Fold the large pieces of fabric and the batting (wadding) in half, lay the straight edge of the template on the fold, and cut out whole mitt pieces. Now lay one long mitt piece right side down, with the batting (wadding) on top, and the other long mitt on top of that, right side up. Lay the small mitts right side up at each end, and pin everything in place—you may also choose to baste (tack) the layers for extra security.

6 Press the rest of the bias binding in half, and cut off a 6-in (15-cm) length. Machine-sew the open edges of this piece and set it aside; it will be the hanging loop. Pin the rest of the bias binding all around the outside edges of the oven mitts, taking extra care around the curves. Fold the ends under and make sure they meet neatly. Position the hanging loop in the center of one edge, tucking the cut ends under the bias binding. With a straight or decorative stitch, sew around the bias binding, removing pins as you go and making sure you sew over the ends of the hanging loop.

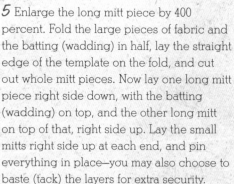

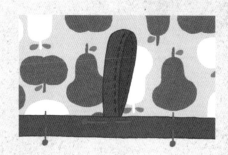

Functional, and fabulous, coasters

The perfect problem solver for tea and coffee ring stains—and they look pretty pleasing, too!

Crafty needs!

2 pieces of fabric measuring 4¹/₂ x 4¹/₂in (11 x 11cm) for each coaster

Pins, needles, and scissors

Sewing machine

Sewing thread to tone with fabric

1 piece of fusible webbing measuring 4 x 4in (10 x 10cm) for each coaster

1 piece of fleece measuring 4 x 4in (10 x 10cm) for each coaster

Iron

1 When cutting the fabric squares, pick out shapes or a motif that will look good. Put the two squares right together and pin. Set the sewing machine to a medium straight stitch (see page 128) and sew around the edges, taking a ½-in (1-cm) seam allowance and leaving an 2-in (5-cm) gap in one side.

2 Lay the fusible webbing centrally on the fabric that will be the bottom of the coaster, then lay the fleece on top of that and iron it in place.

3 Snip the corners of the square diagonally (see page 130) so that they will be pointy when you turn the coaster right side out.

4 Turn the coaster right side out and press, pressing under the seam allowances across the gap. Topstitch (see page 129) around the coaster with a contrast thread.

Use different fabrics to make a whole collection of coasters—and may you drink tea happily ever after.

Cuddly companions

The not-at-all-folly dolly girl

Dolls are one of my favorite makes. It's always exciting to see how they evolve into little characters. Perfect for children, and the child inside of you!

1 Enlarge the templates by 200 percent and cut out four arms and four legs, two heads, two dresses, and one of each of the hair pieces. If the skin fabric has a right and a wrong side, remember to flip the templates over to make left and right arms and legs.

2 Let's start with the arms and legs. Pin two matching pieces right sides together. Set the sewing machine to a medium straight stitch (see page 128), and sew around the edge, taking a ¼-in (5-mm) seam allowance and leaving the square end open. Turn each arm and leg right side out, and stuff them lightly with toy stuffing. Set these aside.

3 Pin the felt front hair in place on the face piece. With embroidery floss (thread), work running stitch (see page 132) along the lower edge of the hair to sew it to the face.

4 Now do the same for the back of the head, then sew on the pigtail pieces, as shown. Tie two lengths of ribbon into bows and hand-stitch one to the top of each pigtail.

stitch snippets

Choose your fabrics carefully. Cotton and soft canvas fabrics work best; make sure they are durable and not too thin. You need plain cream or pale pink fabric for the face and arms and legs and a pretty patterned fabric for the dress. The doll's hair is made from felt, as are her cheeks.

Crafty needs!

- Templates on page 137
- Fabrics and felts (see stitch snippets)
- Iron
- Pins, needles, and scissors
- Sewing machine
- Sewing threads to tone with fabrics
- Toy stuffing
- Brown felt for hair and orange for cheeks
- Embroidery flosses (threads)
- Ribbon for hair bows
- Fading fabric marker
- Buttons for eyes and to decorate dress

5 Draw the eyes, nose, and mouth onto the face with the fading fabric marker (see page 128). Using embroidery flosses (threads) and running stitch or backstitch (see page 132)—whichever you prefer—stitch over the lines. Cut circles of felt for the rosy cheeks and sew them in place with straight stitches (see page 132). Sew on buttons for the eyes.

6 Right sides together and matching the necks, pin the face to one dress piece. Sew along the neck seam, taking a ½-in (1-cm) seam allowance. Repeat with the back of the head and the other dress piece. Then press the seams open. Sew buttons to the front of the dress for decoration.

7 Find the arms and legs you made first of all. Baste (tack) the arms to the right side of the front dress piece, facing inward and with the tops at the position of the shoulders. Baste (tack) the legs to the dress, with the tops aligned with the hem and the feet facing toward the head. It all looks odd at the moment, but when the doll is turned and stuffed, the arms and legs will stick out.

8 Once the arms and legs are basted (tacked) into position, place the back body piece on top of the front, so that the right sides are facing each other. Make sure all the limbs, the pigtails, and ribbons are tucked in (this can be a bit tricky), and pin in place. Sew around the head and body, taking a ½-in (1-cm) seam allowance and leaving an opening in one side that's big enough to fit all the limbs through. Notch all the curves (see page 130) so they don't pucker and turn the doll right side out. Fill her with toy stuffing and slip stitch (see page 132) the opening shut.

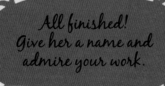

All finished! Give her a name and admire your work.

The not-at-all-folly dolly boy

The boy is made in very much the same way as the girl on page 32, apart from the clothes he wears.

1 Enlarge the templates by 200 percent. Cut out two trouser shapes, four shirt sleeves, and two shirt torsos. Cut two heads, four hands, four feet, and one each of the hair pieces.

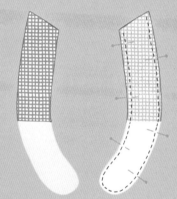

2 Right sides together, pin a hand to the end of each sleeve and sew the seams, taking a ½-in (1-cm) seam allowance. Press the seam allowances open. Pair up the arms right sides together and sew around the edges, leaving the straight top edge open. Turn right side out and stuff each arm.

Crafty needs!

- Fabric and felt for doll and clothes
- Templates on pages 137 and 138
- Buttons for eyes and to decorate shirt
- Orange felt for hair
- Plus the equipment needed to make the girl doll

3 Right sides together, pin then baste (tack) a foot to the bottom of each trouser leg. Fold the foot out flat and press the seam allowances upward. Topstitch (see page 129) across the bottom of the trousers, ¼in (5mm) up from the bottom edge, sewing through all layers. Take out the basting (tacking) stitches.

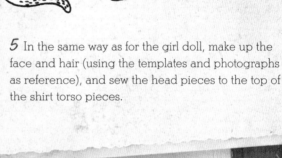

4 Right sides facing, pin a trouser piece to a shirt piece, matching the bottom of the shirt to the top of the trousers. Taking a ½-in (1-cm) seam allowance, machine-sew the seam, then press the seam open. Repeat with the other trouser and shirt pieces. Sew buttons onto the right side of the shirt front.

5 In the same way as for the girl doll, make up the face and hair (using the templates and photographs as reference), and sew the head pieces to the top of the shirt torso pieces.

6 Baste (tack) the arms to the right side of the shoulders of the shirt torso, in the same way as for the girl doll. Pin the doll front and back right sides together. Be careful to match the seams at the neck, waist, and ankles. Taking a ½-in (1-cm) seam allowance, sew all around the edges, leaving a gap for turning through. Turn the doll right side out and stuff it, then slip stitch (see page 132) the gap closed.

Cordelia the curious owl pillow

This project combines three of my favorite things; owls, color, and pillows. Put them all together, and out pops Cordelia the curious owl. She's fun to make and looks pretty wherever she perches.

Crafty needs!

16-in (40-cm) round pillow form (cushion pad)

Plain cotton fabric for the front and back

Pins, needles, and scissors

Sewing machine

Sewing threads to tone with fabrics

7 different patterned fabrics for the front

Templates on page 138

Felts in various colors

Iron

Glue (optional)

Embroidery floss (thread)

Toy stuffing

1 Measure the pillow form (cushion pad) and add ½-in (1-cm) seam allowance around the perimeter. Cut out a circle this size from the plain cotton fabric. Then cut out two part-circles, each two-thirds of the size of the front piece, for the back envelope opening; remember to cut a left-hand and a right-hand piece. On the straight edge of each back piece, fold over a double ¼-in (5-mm) hem and press then pin. With the feed dogs up, set the sewing machine to a medium straight stitch (see page 128) and sew the hems, close to the folded-over edge. Set these back pieces aside.

2 From patterned fabric, cut a semi-circle half the size of the front circle. Enlarge the feather templates by 400 percent and cut the six rows of feathers from different fabrics (the different rows are marked by dotted lines: the longest is the top row, the shortest the bottom row). Cut the same feather pieces from neutral-colored felt. Enlarge the remaining templates by 200 percent and cut four wings, one outer eye, two each of the inner eyes, two feet and one beak from felts. Iron all the pieces.

3 Wrong sides together, pin each patterned feather piece to its coordinating felt piece. Set the sewing machine to a medium zigzag stitch and sew along the scalloped edge to stop it from fraying and to add detail.

4 Right sides together and matching the straight edges, pin the patterned semi-circle to the top row of feathers. Set the sewing machine to a medium straight stitch and sew along the straight edge, taking a ½-in (1-cm) seam allowance. Fold the feathers down and press the seam flat. Lay this piece on the plain cotton front circle, matching the curves, and pin it at the top to keep it in place to use as a size guide.

5 Fold the first row of feathers up so it is right side down on the half circle. Right side down, position the next row of feathers (the next size down) under the first row, about 1in (2.5cm) lower down the plain cotton circle. Sew the straight edge of second row of feathers to the plain cotton circle. Fold the second row back down and press the seam flat. Repeat this with the next four rows of feathers, so that they cover the plain cotton circle.

6 Then position the owl's eyes and beak on the patterned top half of the front and pin or glue them in place (see page 128). Using embroidery floss (thread), straight stitch (see page 132) around all the eye pieces. Machine-sew around the edge of the beak with a straight stitch.

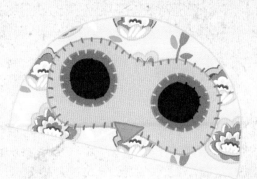

7 Right sides together, pin the four wing pieces into pairs. Machine-sew around the outside edge, taking a ½-in (1-cm) seam allowance and leaving the straight edge open. Clip the seam allowances around the curves (see page 130), then turn the wings right sides out and press. Stuff the wings lightly, then take them back to the sewing machine and sew curved lines from the scalloped edge to the straight edge, three lines on each wing.

8 Now lay the front of the owl flat and right side up. Position a wing on either side of the owl, facing inward and with the straight edges against the edges of the owl's front. Pin the wings in place. Position the felt feet at the bottom in the same way and pin.

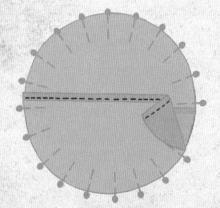

9 Then lay the two back pieces right sides down on top, so that the hemmed edges run horizontally across the owl: the bottom hemmed edge should overlap the top hemmed edge. Pin the layers together all the way around. Taking a ½-in (1-cm) seam allowance, machine-sew right around the edge of the cover. Trim the seam allowances and cut notches in the curves (see page 130) to keep the edges from puckering too much. Turn the owl right side out and insert the pillow form (cushion pad) into the envelope opening at the back.

Bonkers bobtail bunnies

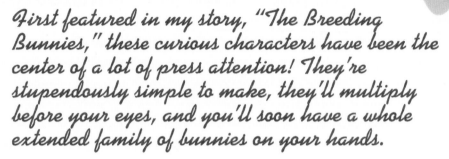

First featured in my story, "The Breeding Bunnies," these curious characters have been the center of a lot of press attention! They're stupendously simple to make, they'll multiply before your eyes, and you'll soon have a whole extended family of bunnies on your hands.

Crafty needs!

Template on page 139

Pins, needles, and scissors

Fabric for body

Felts for eyes, nose, and ears

Fabric glue (optional)

Embroidery floss (thread)

Buttons

Sewing machine with embroidery foot

Sewing threads in colors of your choice

Toy stuffing

Wool tops

Ribbon

Add a ribbon around the bunny's neck and tie in a bow so your bunny looks dapper!

1 Enlarge the template by 400 percent and cut out two bunny shapes, with a ½-in (1-cm) seam allowance added all around, from the main fabric (see page 128). Cut two eye shapes, two inner ear shapes, and a small triangle for the nose out of felt in colors of your choice. Pin or glue the eyes, ears, and nose in place (see page 128) on one of the body pieces.

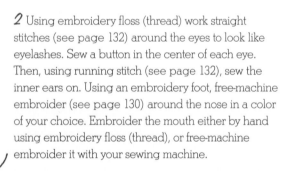

2 Using embroidery floss (thread) work straight stitches (see page 132) around the eyes to look like eyelashes. Sew a button in the center of each eye. Then, using running stitch (see page 132), sew the inner ears on. Using an embroidery foot, free-machine embroider (see page 130) around the nose in a color of your choice. Embroider the mouth either by hand using embroidery floss (thread), or free-machine embroider it with your sewing machine.

3 Pin the bunny pieces right sides together. With the feed dogs up, set the sewing machine to a medium straight stitch (see page 128) and, taking a ½-in (1-cm) seam allowance, sew around the edge, leaving a gap in one side for turning through.

4 Snip small notches out of the seam allowance around the curves and at the corners of the bunny (see page 130), being careful not to cut the stitching.

5 Turn the bunny right side out and stuff it. Slip stitch (see page 132) the gap closed. Roll some wool tops tightly into a ball to make the tail and, using matching thread, sew it to the back of the bunny.

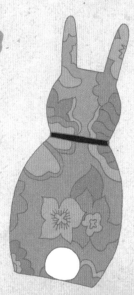

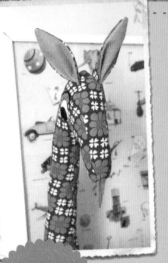

George the giraffe

Meet George: he's a good-natured giraffe, but a little shy. He's going through a bit of an awkward, gangly stage, so he needs someone to love him and watch him blossom into a confident adult giraffe.

Templates on page 139

Fabric for body

Pins, needles, and scissors

Pink cotton for the tongue

Black, white, and pink felt for the eyes and ears

Iron

Fabric glue (optional)

Fading fabric marker

Black embroidery floss (thread)

Sewing machine

Sewing threads to tone with fabrics

Modeling wire or pipe cleaner for the tail

Stuffing

Pom-pom, or brown yarn and thick card to make your own (see page 131)

1 Enlarge the body template by 600 percent (you'll need to do this in sections and tape them together) and the other templates by 400 percent, and cut out all the shapes (see page 128). From printed fabric, cut two bodies, two underbodies, two ears, and one head gusset. Cut two tongues from pink cotton fabric. From pink felt cut two more ears. Cut the outer eyes from white felt and the inner eyes from black felt. Cut two printed fabric strips measuring 10½ x 1½in (27 x 3.5cm) for the tail.

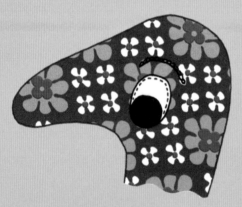

2 Glue or pin the smaller black eye circle onto the larger white eye circle, then glue or pin these (see page 128) onto either side of the giraffe's head, making sure they line up. Hand-sew straight stitches (see page 132) around the perimeter using matching threads. Draw an eyebrow above each eye with the fading fabric marker, and with black embroidery floss (thread), chain stitch (see page 132) over the lines.

3 Pin each felt ear piece right sides together to a fabric ear piece. Set the sewing machine to a small straight stitch (see page 128) and, taking a ½-in (1-cm) seam allowance, sew along each side, leaving an opening in the bottom. Turn each ear right side out and press it. Then fold the ears into a concertina shape, as shown.

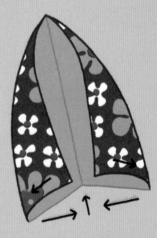

4 Right sides together, pin the underbody pieces to the main body pieces. Taking a ½-in (1-cm) seam allowance, machine-sew each underbody in place around the legs, leaving the top straight edge open.

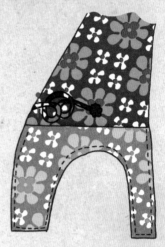

5 Pin the two tail pieces right sides together and, taking a ½-in (1-cm) seam allowance, machine-sew around the edges, leaving one short end open. Turn the tail right side out through the opening and stuff it. Then thread a thin piece of modeling wire or pipe cleaner through the tail, which you'll bend into a corkscrew shape a bit later. Pin the tail in place, so it's inside the giraffe's body.

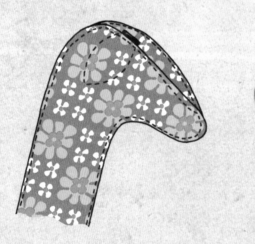

6 Next, lay the main body pieces right sides together. Pin the ears to the right side of one end of the head gusset, with the felt inners facing forward. Then pin the head gusset in position on the main body pieces, making sure that the right side of the fabric is facing inward and the ears are hanging down inside the body. Now, starting from the top of the legs where the underbody stitching ends and taking a ½-in (1-cm) seam allowance, sew around the body and up the neck to the head gusset. Sew around one side of the gusset and fasten off. Go back to the other side of the gusset and sew around it, then continue around the rest of the head and down to the other side of the underbody.

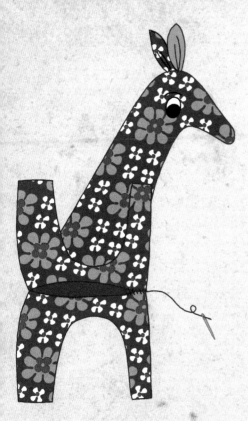

7 Turn everything right side out. Stuff the legs and neck tightly so that they will stand up straight, but stuff the nose lightly so that the mouth can be pushed in later, then slip stitch (see page 132) the tummy closed.

8 Machine-sew the tongue pieces right sides together, leaving the straight end open. Turn the tongue right side out and press it. Hand-sew the tongue to the end of the nose, then push the very end of the nose in on itself to make a mouth (a stitch or two might be needed to hold it in place). For the finishing touch, curl the giraffe's tail into a corkscrew shape and hand-sew a pom-pom to the end.

Your giraffe is ready to roam your room.

Cute-as-a-kitten doorstop

We have swingy doors at home; every time one door opens another slams shut. We also have Jake the cat, who likes to be in whichever room is shut and won't stop meowing until it's opened. The perfect solution? A cat doorstop!

1 Enlarge the template by 400 percent and cut out a cat body (see page 128). Flip the template over and cut out another shape, so that you have a back and a front. Also cut out a tail from different fabric and the eyes from felt.

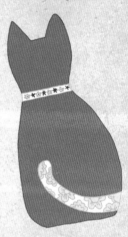

2 Position a length of ribbon across the cat's neck on both pieces of body fabric, making sure they match up when the pieces are put together, and pin or glue them in place (see page 128). Pin or glue the tail to the front cat piece, with the square end aligned with the edge of the body.

3 Draw on the face with the fabric marker and glue on the felt eyes. Free-machine embroider (see page 130) the features in a contrasting color, and stitch around the eyes in white. Sew along the edges of the ribbon and around the tail. Sew on buttons for the pupils, then using embroidery floss (thread), satin stitch (see page 132) the nose.

4 Pin the front and back of the cat right sides together. With the feed dogs up, set the sewing machine to a medium straight stitch (see page 128) and, taking a ½-in (1-cm) seam allowance, sew around the edge. Leave a gap in one side large enough to stuff the cat. Turn right side out.

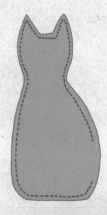

5 Fill a freezer bag with sand, though beans or lentils work well, too. The freezer bag will stop any leaks and protect the fabric. Stuff the top half of the cat, then push in the bag of sand. Add a bit more stuffing around the bag to fill out the body. Slip stitch (see page 132) the gap closed and sew a bell to the collar.

Gifts

Cute and quirky pom-pom skirt

This skirt is fun to make in all sizes—but miniature is the cutest.

Crafty needs!

A rectangle of fabric to fit your chosen child, the circumference of their tummy (or hips, whichever is fatter!) by the desired length of the skirt plus 1¹⁄₄in (2.5cm) for hems

Iron

Pom-pom trim to fit along long edge of fabric

Pins, needles, and scissors

Sewing machine with zigzag foot

Sewing thread to match fabric

Elastic to fit around child's waist

Safety pin

Felt and buttons for flowers (optional)

1 Turn under and press a ½-in (1-cm) hem along the long bottom edge of the fabric. Pin the pom-pom trim to the hem on the wrong side, so that the bobbles hang below the folded edge of the fabric. Set the sewing machine to a medium straight stitch (see page 128) and sew the hem, sewing on the trim at the same time.

2 Right side together, fold the rectangle so that the two short sides meet. Make sure the bottom edge matches up neatly. Machine-sew the seam with a zigzag stitch, or an overcast stitch if your machine has one.

3 Now fold under the top edge by ¼in (5mm) and machine-sew a straight stitch all around. Fold the edge under again, but this time by ½-in (1-cm). Sew around very close to the lower edge, leaving a ½in (1cm) gap close to the seam to thread the elastic through.

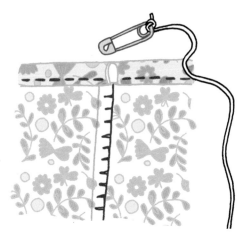

4 Tie a safety pin to one end of the elastic to make it easier to thread through the channel. Thread the elastic through, keeping hold of one end. When the safety pin emerges again, match the ends (making sure the elastic isn't twisted inside the channel), and hand-sew them together, going back and forth a few times for extra strength. Slip stitch (see page 132) the gap closed and you're done!

Decorate your skirt further with felt flowers. Use the templates on page 140 and make up the flowers as for the coat hanger covers on page 70.

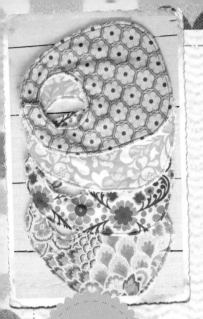

Beautiful baby bib

Babies tend to dribble a lot, and what better way to solve a sticky situation than a beautiful and super-absorbent bib? Save the pennies in style with this fun and functional project, which also makes for a very special baby shower gift.

Crafty needs!

Template on page 140

Fabric for the front

Toweling fabric for the back

Pins, needles, and scissors

Sewing machine

Sewing thread to match fabric

Iron

Snap fastener

Fading fabric marker

1 Enlarge the template by 400 percent. Cut it out and check the size on the baby, adding a little extra to the ends of the straps if need be. Pin the pattern to the fabrics and cut out the front from fabric and the back from the toweling. If you are making several bibs, set up a mini production line and do all the cutting out first, then all the sewing.

2 Pin the pieces right sides together. Set the sewing machine to a medium straight stitch (see page 128) and, taking a ½-in (1-cm) seam allowance, sew around the bib, leaving a 3-in (8-cm) gap at the middle of the neck for turning through.

3 Turn the bib right side out and iron it, pressing under the seam allowances across the gap. Slip stitch (see page 132) the gap closed. Topstitch (see page 129) around the edges of the bib.

Finished!
Your baby will be the cutest in the land. You could also try adding different trims around the edges of the bib, or sewing an appliqué design to the front.

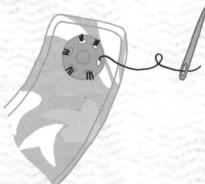

4 Then mark the position of the snap fastener on the strap and sew it on securely with matching thread, making sure that the ball of the snap is on the upper end of the strap and the socket of the snap on the lower end.

Springtime showers mobile

Decorate your home or baby's cot with all things spring-like with this colorful mobile. Remember to hang a mobile out of reach of little fingers, but well within the sight of little eyes.

1 Let's start with the butterflies. For each butterfly you will need a front and a back—and as the butterfly is not symmetrical you will need to cut out one, then flip the template over for the other side (see page 128). Cut a front and back in the same color felt for each of nine butterflies.

2 From fabric scraps of your choice cut out the wing markings—four on each side of each butterfly, so 72 in total. Glue these shapes onto the wings with fabric glue (see page 128). Using contrasting sewing threads, free-machine embroider (see page 130) around the shapes. When you've finished that, embellish each wing with beads and sequins sewn on by hand. Then glue the front and back of each butterfly together and set them aside to dry.

3 Next, cut out all the flower shapes. Again, each of the nine flowers has two sides, and on each side there is a circle center and a smaller flower in the middle. So you'll need to cut 18 large flowers, 18 circles, and 18 small flowers. Glue the circle to the center of each large flower, and the small flower to the center of the circle. With embroidery floss (thread), hand-sew running stitch (see page 132) around each circle and sew a button to the center of each small flower. Then glue the front and back of each flower together and set them aside.

4 Then you need to make three clouds with dangling raindrops (see Raincloud Brooch project on page 82 for instructions).

5 Now, take a 50-in (125-cm) length of embroidery floss (thread) and tie a knot at one (the bottom) end. Using a long needle, thread four beads onto the floss (thread) and slide them down to the knot. Then thread on a butterfly by pushing the needle in and out through the middle of the butterfly several times, as if working running stitch. Thread on a felt ball, then thread on a flower by pushing the needle through the center between the two layers of felt. Space the elements out so that they look good. Continue in this way, threading on a felt ball, a butterfly, a felt ball, a flower, a felt ball, a butterfly, a felt ball, a flower, a felt ball, and finally a rain cloud.

6 You may need to slide each element up or down the floss (thread) to find the perfect composition, and you should have about 8in (20cm) of embroidery floss (thread) left bare at the top. Repeat the process with the other two lengths of floss (thread) and remaining elements to make three decorated strands.

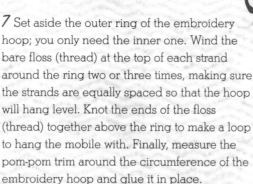

7 Set aside the outer ring of the embroidery hoop; you only need the inner one. Wind the bare floss (thread) at the top of each strand around the ring two or three times, making sure the strands are equally spaced so that the hoop will hang level. Knot the ends of the floss (thread) together above the ring to make a loop to hang the mobile with. Finally, measure the pom-pom trim around the circumference of the embroidery hoop and glue it in place.

Raindrops and rainbows mini quilt

This quilt is ideal for beginners to make and a little bit different from the usual quilt designs you see. Using a very simple appliqué technique, you can create a clever and lovely design that is perfect for snuggling under on cold and rainy days.

1 First select the fabrics you want to use. You need blue for the sky and a selection ranging from reds, pinks, and oranges, through yellows, greens, and blues for the rainbow strips: you'll need ten different fabrics in total. A heavyweight natural cotton works well for the backing. Cut out everything to the sizes required and iron the pieces so you're ready to start.

2 Begin with the rainbow strips. Lay them out in the color order you want them to appear on the quilt (from the red end of the spectrum to the green end). Pin the first two strips right sides together. Set the sewing machine to a medium straight stitch (see page 128) and, taking a ¼-in (5-mm) seam allowance, sew the seam down one long edge—you need to be as accurate as you can here. Repeat the process with the next pair of strips and continue so you have five double-width strips. Press all the seams flat.

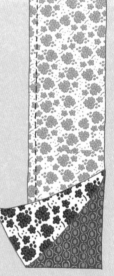

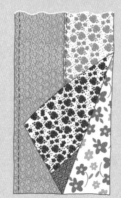

3 Repeat the process to sew the first double-width strip to the next one, and so on until you have a single, striped piece of fabric. Press all the seams flat again. You've made a rainbow!

4 Enlarge the templates by 200 percent; I used one cloud from the mobile project (see page 56). Draw the clouds and six raindrops on the wrong side of the white fabric, then cut out the shapes to rough squares. Pin the right side of the squares to the fusible side of the interfacing, then machine sew around the drawn lines. Trim the seam allowances and cut notches around the curves (see page 130) to stop the seams from puckering. Snip an opening in the middle of the interfacing and turn each piece right side out.

5 Position the clouds and raindrops right sides up on the sky fabric (so the fusible side of the interfacing is against the blue fabric), and iron in place. You may need to also use pins to hold the pieces in place for stitching. Then using white thread, slip stitch (see page 132) around each cloud and raindrop.

Tea break! And I come back to find Jake testing the half-made quilt.

6 Once Jake has been removed from his comfy new bed, the next step is to attach the sky to the rainbow. Right sides together, pin the pieced rainbow section to the bottom edge of the appliquéd sky section. Make sure all the seam allowances of the rainbow are flat and there is no puckering in either piece of fabric. Taking a ¼-in (5-mm) seam allowance, sew the seam then press it flat.

Lay the front of the quilt on a flat surface right side up and gently pull it square and taut by sticking little pieces of masking tape all around the edges, smoothing out any wrinkles in the fabric as you go. On top of this lay the backing of the quilt right side down, and finally lay the batting (wadding) on top.

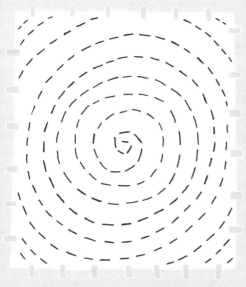

7 Now, using either curved quilting pins (or a curved sewing needle and contrasting thread), pin (or baste/tack long stitches) through all three layers of the fabric. Start in the center and spiral outward, smoothing out wrinkles and puckers as you go. Then pin around each edge of the quilt.

8 Remove the tape and sew along each edge, taking a ½-in (1-cm) seam allowance and leaving a 6-in (15-cm) gap for turning through. Remove the pins or basting (tacking) stitches. Snip off the corners and trim any unruly edges and turn the quilt right side out. Slip stitch (see page 132) the gap closed, and there you have it!

Try making different-sized quilts and be creative with designs and color palettes.

Pins and needles case

Don't get in a muddle with your sewing stuff; instead, make a perfectly practical case and store pins and needles in style!

1 Cut an 8¼ x 5in (21 x 12.5cm) outer case from felt and one from interfacing. Cut an 8¾ x 5½in (22 x 13.5cm) lining from fabric. Cut a 7¼ x 4½in (18.5 x 11.25cm) rectangle for the "pages" from felt, and trim the edges with pinking shears for a decorative finish. Cut 4¼ x 3¼in (10.5 x 8.5cm) rectangles of fabric and interfacing for the front panel. Enlarge the templates by 200 percent and cut the apple shape from red fabric and from interfacing, and the green leaf and the white highlight from felt.

Crafty needs!

Fabrics and felts

Iron-on interfacing

Ruler

Templates on page 140

Fading fabric marker

Pins, needles, and scissors

Pinking shears

Iron

Sewing machine with embroidery foot

Sewing threads to match felts and fabrics

Fabric glue (optional)

2 Fold under each edge of the lining piece by ¼in (5mm) and press. Miter the corners, then sandwich the appropriate piece of interfacing between the felt outer case and the lining and pin in place. Set the sewing machine to a medium straight stitch (see page 128) and sew all the way around, ¼in (5mm) in from the edge.

3 Match the front panel piece to its interfacing piece and iron them together. Trim the edges with pinking shears. Iron the apple to its interfacing and pin or glue (see page 128) it to the front of the rectangle. Add the leaf and the white highlight, and draw a stalk with the fabric marker. Then free-machine embroider (see page 130) around the apple and leaf in matching threads. Embroider the stalk with brown thread by going back and forth with the sewing machine.

4 Fold the case in half and press it. Do the same to the felt "pages" piece with the pinked edge. Position the "pages" inside the case so that the folds meet, close the case, and pin the layers together. With the feed dogs up, set the sewing machine to a medium straight stitch and sew down the front of the needle case, sewing ¼in (5mm) in from the folded edge.

5 Position the front rectangle fabric with the apple design on the front of the needle case and pin it in place. Machine-sew around the edge; make sure the bobbin thread matches the lining fabric so that it blends in nicely.

Congratulations— you just made a very stylish pins and needles case. Try out different designs, add buttons, beads, sequins, and trims, and have lots of fun!

One-of-a-kind book cover

If, like me, you get through notebooks at a furious rate, you know how expensive it is to buy pretty ones. Instead, stock up on cheap ones and design your own covers! Felt is good for a first cover, as it won't fray. Once you are a confident cover-maker, you can use pretty patterned fabrics.

1 Open the notebook out, lay it flat and measure it. Measure from the edge of the front cover across the spine to the edge of the back cover, and from the top edge to the bottom edge. Add 4in (10cm) to each side and ½in (1cm) to the top and the bottom. Cut a rectangle of felt to these measurements.

If you're using a fabric other than felt, you may want to iron on interfacing and sew the edges of the fabric with a zigzag stitch on the sewing machine to stop the fabric from fraying.

2 Fold under a ¼-in (5-mm) hem on each side edge and press. Repeat with the top and bottom edges. Trim away a bit of felt at each corner to make a miter and reduce the bulk. Using the sewing machine and matching thread, zigzag stitch right around the hemmed edges.

3 Fold in the sides by 3½in (9cm) and press. Then open the folds out again to decorate the cover.

4 Choose a design: it could be a picture or even just a word. For this robin design, you'll need the bird template from the tea towel (see page 14), white felt, red fabric for the breast, and brown fabric for the wing. Enlarge the template to suit your notebook and draw around the pieces onto the fabrics with the fading marker. Cut out the fabric pieces.

5 Collage the design onto the felt, positioning it so that it will appear on the front of the notebook. When you're pleased with it, lightly glue the pieces in place with fabric glue (see page 128).

6 Free-machine embroider (see page 130) around the bird with black thread, adding an eye and legs. Color in the beak with stitches in yellow thread, then go around the bird several times with different-colored threads: I've used yellow, turquoise, and brown.

7 When you've done that, fold in the sides again along the creases you ironed earlier and pin the folds in place. With the feed dogs up, set the sewing machine to a medium straight stitch (see page 128) and sew a ¼-in (5-mm) seam along the top and bottom of each folded section, reversing at each end to secure the threads. Pop your cheap notebook into your lovely cover.

Snazzy coat hanger cover

We like pretty clothes, so why not have pretty hangers for them? Wire hangers are ugly and get tangled in your wardrobe, so dress them up with tangle-proof covers, and they are a peachy gift! The flower cover is shown here, with other designs for inspiration.

Crafty needs!

Wire coat hanger

Felt to cover the hanger

Fading fabric marker

Tape measure

Pins, needles, and scissors

Templates on page 140

Scraps of colored felts

Sewing machine with zigzag foot and embroidery foot

Sewing threads in green and to match fabrics

Fabric glue

Buttons

Embroidery floss (thread)

Trim

1 Lay the hanger on the felt and draw around it with the fabric marker (don't draw around the hook). Add a ½-in (1-cm) seam allowance to the sides and 1in (2cm) to the bottom edge. If you are using a fraying fabric rather than felt, add another ½in (1cm) to the bottom edge. Cut out two pieces the same.

2 Enlarge the templates by 200 percent and cut out flowers in colors you like. Cut a small circle of yellow felt for the bee. Arrange the flowers on one cover piece at varying heights, but not too close to the top. Draw in the flower stalks with the fabric marker, then remove the flowers. Set the sewing machine to an embroidery stitch and sew along the lines. If you don't have embroidery stitches, a simple zigzag stitch will work nicely, as will chain stitch (see page 132) with embroidery floss (thread).

3 With fabric glue, lightly stick a large flower to the top of each stem (see page 128), and place a smaller flower on top. Sew a button into the middle of each flower, sewing through all the layers of felt, including the cover piece.

4 With the fabric marker, draw a wriggly line as if the bee has flown from flower to flower. With embroidery floss (thread), work running stitch (see page 132) over the line. Glue the felt bee to the end of the line. With the sewing machine and black thread, zigzag a stripe and free-machine embroider (see page 130) wings. Embroider the eye and smile with hand stitches.

5 At the top of both cover pieces (where the hook will come through), fold under and press a ½-in (1-cm) hem. Snip notches in the hem allowance to stop the fabric from puckering (see page 130), then sew the hem by hand or with the machine, whichever you prefer.

6 Carefully pin a length of trim along the bottom edge of each cover piece. With matching sewing thread and running stitch, sew the trim in place, removing the pins as you go. (If you use a fabric other than felt for the cover, sew a ½-in (1-cm) hem along the bottom edge to stop it from fraying before adding your trim.)

7 Pin the cover pieces right sides together. Set the sewing machine to a medium straight stitch (see page 128) and, taking a ½-in (1-cm) seam allowance, sew along the two sloping sides. Turn right side out.

Pillowcase tote bag

Replace plastic bags with this cute shopping tote. This is eco-friendly, a simple project to make, and the perfect way to clear out the linen closet. So you're going green, making your friends green with envy, and saving the green stuff (money, not cabbages), all at the same time.

Crafty needs!

1 pillowcase

Pins, needles, and scissors

Iron

Tape measure

Sewing threads to match fabrics

Sewing machine with zigzag foot and embroidery foot

Templates on page 141

Black, white, and pink felts and scraps of fabric for appliqués

Fabric glue

1 Find an old pillowcase, most of us have at least one buried at the bottom of a pile of bed linen. If you really don't have one, a visit to a thrift store is bound to unearth something ideal. Cut off the flap of fabric inside the top of the pillowcase—the bit that holds the pillow in; this will be used for the handles. Fold the pillow in half so that the two short ends meet; this will be the size of your bag. Press the fold to mark it.

2 From the fabric cut off in Step 1, cut two strips about 3½ x 18in (9 x 45cm). Precise measurements depend on the pillowcase size; if you have two pillowcases, you can cut longer handles from the other one. Right side together, fold each strip in half lengthwise. Set the sewing machine to a medium straight stitch (see page 128) and, taking a ½-in (1-cm) seam allowance, sew along the open edge. Turn the handles right side out and press.

3 Lay the pillowcase right side down. Press under a 1-in (2.5-cm) hem along the top long edge. Using the fold pressed in Step 1 to define the front and back of the bag, slip the raw ends of the handles into the pressed hem, one handle on the front and one on the back. Making sure the handles are not twisted, position the ends about 3in (8cm) in from the edges of the front and back, and pin in place. Now the handles look upside down, so fold them up over the hem so they stick out above the bag and re-pin.

4 Machine-sew along the top of the hem, sewing across the handles. Start to sew along the lower edge of the hem. When you reach the base of each handle, pivot the presser foot around and stitch a criss-cross, as shown, to give extra strength.

5 Now for the appliqué design: I have chosen a cat playing with butterflies. Enlarge the templates by 200 percent and cut out all the cat shapes from felts and the ribbon from fabric (see page 128). Cut the butterflies from felt and scraps of patterned fabric. Collage the pieces together on the front of the bag and lightly glue them in place (see page 128). Free-machine embroider (see page 130) around the edges of the pieces, using white thread to define the front and back legs, whiskers, and teeth of the cat, and black thread for the butterfly antennae.

6 Finally, fold the pillowcase right sides together along the line pressed in Step 1. Pin the side and bottom edges and sew along them with a machine zigzag or overcasting stitch. Turn right side out again, and you've done it!

As a reward I think you should go and buy lots of pretty things to put inside your new bag. Well, you need to test it out, don't you?!

Lush and Lavish Laptop Cover

Laptops, iPads, Kindles…they're all great and a work and leisure necessity for many of us these days. So, the perfect way to jazz yours up? This fantabulous funky laptop sleeve! It also protects from bumps and scratches, so it's not only beautiful but practical, too!

Crafty needs!

Tape measure

Paper for pattern

Pencil

Pins, needles, and scissors

Main fabric plus fabric scraps for appliqué design

Batting (wadding) or fleece fabric

Lining fabric

Iron

Template on page 141

Fabric glue

Sewing threads to match fabrics and lining

Sewing machine with embroidery foot and optional buttonhole foot

2 buttons

1 Measure the length and width of your laptop; if it's quite deep, measure that, too. Cut a paper pattern that is the length plus the depth plus 1in (2cm) total seam allowance, by the width plus the depth plus 1in (2cm) total seam allowance.

Then draw a pattern for the straps; an oblong shape with one rounded end works nicely, but feel free to change it to suit your tastes. Add ¼in (5mm) seam allowances all around.

Next, cut out all the pieces. For the case you'll need two pieces in the main fabric, two in the batting (wadding) or fleece, and two in the lining fabric. Cut the same fabrics for the straps, cutting one piece for each of the two straps.

Use exactly the same principles to cut pieces for a case for any other bit of electronic kit you want to protect. Small items might need just one strap.

2 Let's start with the straps. For each one, place the main fabric on top of the lining right sides together, and place the batting (wadding)/fleece on top of that. Pin the layers together. With the feed dogs up, set the sewing machine to a medium straight stitch (see page 128) and, taking a ¼-in (5-mm) seam allowance, sew around the edge, leaving the bottom straight edge open. Turn the straps right side out, so that the batting (wadding) is between the lining and main fabric, and give them an iron if they need it.

3 To add a nice detail, topstitch (see page 129) around the edge of each strap. Sew on the right side, with thread to match the main fabric on the top spool and thread to match the lining on the bobbin; this ensures that the topstitching blends in with the fabrics on both sides of the strap. If you have an automatic buttonhole feature on your sewing machine, use that and a buttonhole foot to sew a buttonhole near the rounded end of each strap. To sew the buttonholes manually use a zigzag foot (see page 130).

4 Next, cut out the motifs for the front of the case, using fabrics of your choice. Add details using scraps of different patterned fabrics. You can copy the tote bag butterfly motifs I've used (see page 141), or create your own design. Collage the pieces together on the right side of one of the main fabric pieces, sticking them in place with fabric glue. Lower the feed dogs on the sewing machine and free-machine embroider (see page 130) around the design in colors of your choice. Hand-sew on any other embellishments you'd like, such as beads or buttons.

Pretty buttons are very pleasing, and there are zillions to choose from. Have fun picking the perfect ones.

5 Pin the two main fabric pieces right sides together. With the feed dogs up, set the sewing machine to a medium straight stitch and, taking a ½-in (1-cm) seam allowance, sew around three sides of the case, leaving one short side open. Snip away excess fabric at the corners so that they have a nice point when turned right side out (see page 130). Turn the case right side out and iron it.

6 Right sides facing, pin and baste (tack) the straps to the open edge of the back piece, matching the raw end of the strap to the raw edge of the fabric. Make sure there's an equal space either side of each strap.

7 Lay one piece of batting (wadding) or fleece flat. On top of this put both lining pieces right sides together, then lay the second batting (wadding) or fleece piece on top of the linings. Make sure all the edges are aligned. In the same way as for the main fabric case, machine sew both long sides and one of the short sides, but leave a 4-in (10-cm) gap in the middle of that short side: leave the other short side completely open. Trim excess fabric at the corners as for the main fabric in Step 5. Do not turn this piece inside out.

8 Right sides together, slip the main piece inside the lining and match the raw edges around the open short end. Pin and then baste (tack) the layers together around the open end, making sure that the straps are tucked down inside and only the raw ends of them are being caught in the stitching. Taking a ½-in (1-cm) seam allowance, machine-sew right around the open top edge.

9 Pull the main fabric out through the gap in the lining piece, and keep pulling through until the lining is turned right side out (this sounds a bit confusing, but when the project is in front of you it will make prefect sense). Slip stitch (see page 132) the gap in the lining closed. Then push the lining back into the main fabric, tucking it in to the corners, and iron the case.

10 Sew two buttons to the front of the case to align with the buttonholes in the straps, then pat yourself on the back!

stitch snippets

Try using different fabrics, colors, and appliqué designs to suit you or whoever you're making a case for.

Raincloud Brooch

Brooches are fun to make and are great for showing your personality in a creative way. You can pin them to your coat, bag, hat, or dress and completely transform an ordinary outfit into something special. You can make your brooches fun, glamorous, cute—whatever suits your mood.

Template on page 140

Crafty needs!

Template on page 140

White felt

Fading fabric marker

Pins, needles, and scissors

6 droplet beads in blue or clear and 6 x 4in (10cm) jewelry chains (alternatively you can use dangly droplet earrings)

Pliers (it's easier with two sets if you have them)

Sewing machine

Sewing thread to match felt

Toy stuffing

Fabric glue (optional)

Brooch finding

1 Enlarge the cloud either from the mobile (see page 56) or the mini quilt (see page 60) to the desired size and cut out two from the white felt. Cut a thin strip of felt the length of the cloud base to sew the raindrops to.

2 Using the pliers, open up the bottom link of one of the chains. It's easier to use one set of pliers to hold the link and one to gently prize the link open, but you can also hold the link with your fingers. Thread a droplet bead onto the open link, then close the link using the pliers. Repeat with each length of chain to make six raindrops.

3 On one long edge of the felt strip, use the fabric marker to mark six spots about ¾in (2cm) apart. Hand-sew the top link of each chain to a marked spot.

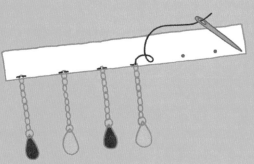

4 Pin the cloud shapes together. Set the sewing machine to a medium straight stitch (see page 128) and sew around the bumpy top edge from one side to the other, but leave the straight bottom open. Stuff the cloud lightly with toy stuffing so it's nice and plump.

5 Next, glue or pin the strip of felt with the raindrops to the inside of the bottom of the cloud. Hand-sew with running stitch (see page 132), or slowly machine-sew, the opening closed. If you use a sewing machine, be extra careful over the chain links so that your needle doesn't break.

6 Finally, mark where the brooch finding should go on the back of the cloud, and hand-sew it on securely, using a needle and white thread.

Pin your brooch to your outfit and you're complete!

Why not try experimenting with some other designs for your fabric brooches. You can use templates from other projects, such as the bird used for the bookcover project (see page 67); a simple felt flower brooch will look great, too.

Rest your weary head

Sleepy head pillow

As the Beatles once sang: "When I wake up in the morning, lift my head, I'm still yawning, when I'm in the middle of a dream, stay in bed, float up stream...."

This is the perfect pillow for all you sleepy heads out there. It's fun and easy to make, and there are a million different designs you could appliqué once you've got the hang of the method.

Measuring tape

Pillow

Fabric for pillowcase

Iron

Pins, needles, and scissors

Sewing machine with zigzag foot

Sewing threads to match fabric and felt

Templates on page 141

Felt for Zs

Fading fabric marker

Fabric glue

1 Start by measuring the length and width of your pillow. The pattern will be: the width, by double the length plus 8in (20cm) for the inside flap. Add ½in (1cm) seam allowance all around. Cut out the pattern from the main fabric.

2 Iron out any creases and lay the fabric right side down. Fold over a double ¼-in (5-mm) hem at one short end of the fabric. Press, and pin in place. Set the sewing machine to a medium straight stitch (see page 128) and sew the hem.

3 At the other end of the fabric, fold over, pin and sew the same double hem. Then fold over 8in (20cm) to the wrong side, press the fold, and pin in place. This will be the flap that holds the pillow inside the case.

4 Enlarge the three templates by 200 percent and cut out the Zs from felt. Turn the pillow fabric right side up and lay it flat, so that the flap is at the right-hand end. Position the Zs on the pillow front, with enough space at one end for your head to lie.

5 Lightly glue or pin (see page 128) the Zs in place. Using a needle and thread, straight stitch (see page 132) the whole way around each letter.

6 Right sides together, fold the fabric so that the hemmed short end meets the folded-over short end. Pin the long edges together, pinning through all layers—including the flap—and making sure there are no creases or puckers in the fabric. With your sewing machine, zigzag stitch the two long edges, leaving the open short edge unstitched. Turn right side out and you're done!

Time for a nap?
ZZZzzzzzzzzzzzzzzzz

Breakfast at Tiffany's eye mask

I love old films, and a favorite is "Breakfast at Tiffany's." Holly Golightly made the little black dress famous, but I adored her sleeping eye mask, and that's the inspiration for this project. Now you can look dazzling even when you're sound asleep!

Crafty needs!

Templates on page 141

Fabric or felt for front, eyelids, and lining

Black felt

Fading fabric marker

Pins, needles, and scissors

Fabric glue

Gold sequins

Gold or yellow sewing thread

Trim for edge of mask

Tape measure

Elastic or ribbon for the tie

Sewing machine

1 Enlarge the templates by 200 percent (see page 141) and cut out two masks, one for the front and one for the lining. Cut out two eyelids from the front fabric and the lusciously long eyelashes from black felt.

2 Position the eyelashes on the bottom of the eyelids, so that they look right, then stick them in place with a dab of fabric glue. Using gold or yellow thread, sew a row of gold sequins along each lash line to glam them up.

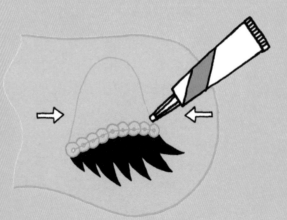

3 Next pinch the edges of the eyelids to mold them into a curved half-cylinder shape. On the back, spread a little glue around the curved edges of each eyelid and stick them onto the front of the eye mask. They should have a slightly 3-D effect.

4 With the fading fabric marker, draw on eyebrows. Using gold or yellow thread, chain stitch (see page 132) the eyebrows. With the same thread, blanket stitch (see page 132) around the curve of each eyelid.

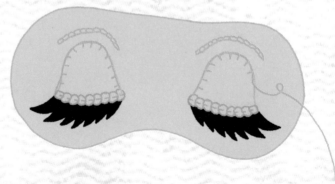

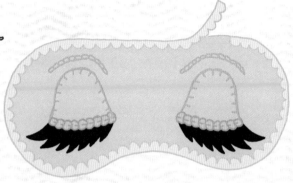

5 Glue or pin (see page 128) the trim all the way around the edge of the decorated front piece, with the shaped edge facing inward. You might need to snip the curves (see page 130) to avoid puckering.

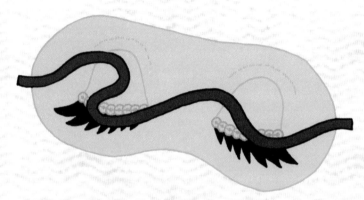

6 If you're using elastic for the tie, measure it around your head from temple to temple, pulling the elastic so that it's taut but not too tight; you want the mask to stay on but not to give you a headache! If you choose ribbon, measure from your temple to the back of your head, then add extra to tie a bow. Cut two pieces to that length. Pin the ends of the elastic or ribbon in position at the sides of the mask.

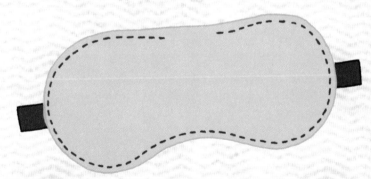

7 Right sides together, pin the mask lining to the mask front. Pin all around the edges, making sure that the loose elastic or ribbon doesn't get caught in the pinning. Set the sewing machine to a medium straight stitch (see page 128) and, taking a ½-in (1-cm) seam allowance, sew around the edge, removing pins as you go and leaving a 3-in (8-cm) gap in the middle of the top edge for turning through. As you get to the ends of the elastic or ribbon, go back and forth over them a couple of times for extra strength. Trim the seam allowance to about half its width and turn the mask right side out. Slip stitch (see page 132) the gap closed. Plump up the eyelids if they need it.

Et voilà! Look a million dollars while you snooze.

Butterfly catcher pillow

I love pillows (cushions), and I think everybody should make at least one in their life time. Hopefully by the end of this book you'll be inspired to make your own all the time. They're super-easy to make, and are a great way to recycle old fabrics (favorite skirts, bed sheets, curtains…). You can put your creations on your sofa, your bed, in your office, and the possibilities for designs are almost endless.

1 Try not to worry about copying my design exactly: be creative with the fabric you choose and let it determine the shapes. Often, the less you worry about getting something technically right and the more adventurous you are, the more unexpected and pleasing the results will be.

I used a 12-in (30-cm) pillow form (cushion pad), but you can use any size—just adjust the fabric sizes to suit. Lightly draw the design on the front fabric piece freehand with a fading fabric marker, or tape the template to a window and trace it off (see page 128). Enlarge the templates by 200 percent and cut out the fabric shapes for the girl and butterflies. Use the flower templates from the coat hanger project (see page 140) and enlarge them to suit. Collage the pieces together on the cushion front and use fabric glue or fusible webbing to hold them in place (see page 128).

2 Now for the bit I like best: free-machine embroidery (see page 130). Outline all the appliqué fabric pieces with stitching, using colors to complement the fabrics, and make the shoes with stitches. Embroider the butterfly net with its long handle and the stems and leaves of the colorful flowers, using the photo as a guide if you wish. I have used a simple straight stitch for most of the design (including the shoes), and a zigzag stitch for the flower petals, but you can use different embroidery stitches if you want to. Sew a button into the center of each flower.

3 On one long edge of each back piece, fold the fabric over ¼in (5mm) and press, then fold it over ½in (1cm) and press again. Pin the hems in place. With the feed dogs up, set the sewing machine to a medium straight stitch (see page 128) and sew the hems. Measure the diameter of the buttons. On one of the back pieces, mark two evenly-spaced buttonholes, each one ¼in (5mm) longer than the measured button size. If you have an automatic buttonhole feature on your sewing machine, use that. If not, sew the buttonholes manually with a zigzag foot (see page 130).

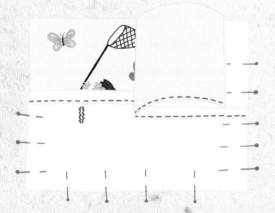
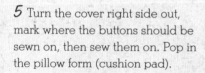

4 Right side up, lay the embroidered front piece flat. Right side down, lay the back piece with buttonholes on top of the front piece, matching the raw edges so that the buttonholes are more or less in the middle. Lay the other back piece right side down on top of this, with the hem overlapping the buttonholes. Taking a ½-in (1-cm) seam allowance, machine sew around all four sides.

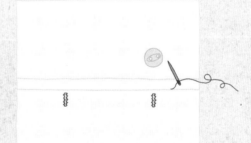

5 Turn the cover right side out, mark where the buttons should be sewn on, then sew them on. Pop in the pillow form (cushion pad).

Let your new creation take pride of place on your sofa and try to keep it away from wily cats like Jake, who wants to make mine his new bed!

Pom-pom-a-licious slippers!

Warm your tootsies with these whimsical slippers. Try out different fabrics and colors and build yourself an extensive pom-pom-a-licious slipper collection.

1 Enlarge the templates by 267 percent. For each slipper, cut out two upper pieces from outer fabric. You'll need to flip the template to cut a left-hand and a right-hand side for each slipper. Cut two uppers from fleece lining, and for the sole cut one piece from fleece and one from thick felt. Iron all the fabrics.

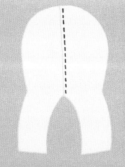

2 Pin the two outer slipper uppers right sides together. Set the sewing machine to a medium straight stitch (see page 128) and, taking a ¼-in (5-mm) seam allowance, sew the seam from the toe to the middle of the slipper. Open the piece out and press the seam open. Repeat this step with the fleece lining uppers.

3 Pin the lining and outer uppers right sides together. Machine-sew around the inner curve, from one side of the heel to the other, taking a ¼-in (5-mm) seam allowance. Clip the curves (see page 130) and turn the joined pieces right side out.

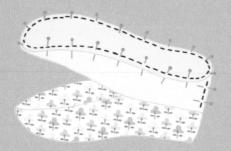

4 Right sides together, pin the sole fleece lining to the upper fleece lining, and pin the heel together. Taking a ¼-in (5-mm) seam allowance, machine-sew the sole in place and sew the heel seam.

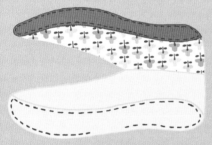

5 Then pin the right side of the felt sole to the right side of the outer slipper, and pin the outer heel. Leaving a 3-in (8-cm) gap in the sole stitching for turning through, sew these seams.

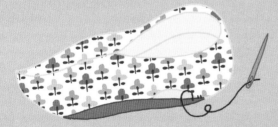

6 Turn everything right sides out through the gap, and stuff the lining into the outer slipper. Slip stitch (see page 132) the gap closed.

7 Then make two pom-poms (see page 131) and hand-sew one to the toe of each slipper.

Fancy fabric bookmarks

Make bedtime reading more special by making your own colorful bookmarks. They are super-fast and easy-peasey to sew, and they make a top-notch gift for an avid reader, too!

Crafty needs!

Fabric

Pins, needles, and scissors

Iron

Mediumweight fusible interfacing

Sewing machine

Sewing thread

Button

Ribbon

1 Cut the fabric to the required size—I made my bookmarks 8¾ x 2½in (22 x 6cm). Iron a piece of interfacing onto the wrong side of the fabric (see page 128). Fold in half, right sides together. Press the fold and pin the edges.

2 Set the sewing machine to a medium straight stitch (see page 128) and, taking a ½-in (1-cm) seam allowance, sew around the edges. Leave a 2-in (5-cm) gap in one short edge. Clip the corners (see page 130) and turn right side out. Press the seam allowances under across the gap, then topstitch (see page 129) around the bookmark.

3 Hand-sew a button to the top of the bookmark, then tie a ribbon around the button.

You're done! Yes, it really is that simple to make something lovely.

Swirly twirly pom-pom pillow

This is where we get really creative with fabric...If you're a bit nervous about color and pattern, this project will really loosen you up!

Crafty needs!

Fabric for pillow (cushion) and lots of different fabrics for appliqué design

Pins, needles, and scissors

Templates on page 134 and 140

Tape measure

16-in (40-cm) round pillow form (cushion pad)

Fading fabric marker

Sewing machine with embroidery foot and optional buttonhole foot

Sewing threads to match main fabric and in lots of colors of your choice

Fabric glue

Beads

Sequins

Buttons for fastening and extras for details

Pom-pom trim

Iron

1 Grab all of your favorite bits of fabric, plonk them in a pile on the floor or a table, then sit down and take the time to really look at them. Is there a section in a piece that really stands out? A flower, a swirly paisley pattern, a butterfly? Look through every piece and get to know the fabrics you have. Cut out all these favorite motifs and put them aside. Whenever I do this, I always turn back to see that Jake has skilfully burrowed himself into the pile and is taking a nap. Ingenious.

2 Use the butterfly from the mobile project (see page 56) and the bird from the tea towel project (see page 14), enlarging them to suit. Cut them out of the appliqué fabrics, making best use of some of the favorite motifs for the birds' tails and butterfly's wings. Detail the cut-out shapes with different patterned fabrics, layer them up until you're happy with them, and glue the elements in together using fabric glue. Then allow to dry.

3 Now measure the pillow form (cushion pad) and cut out a circle from the main fabric, adding ½in (1cm) seam allowance around the perimeter. Then cut out two semi-circles two-thirds of the size of the front piece for the envelope opening; remember to cut a left-hand and a right-hand piece. On the straight edge of each back piece, fold the over a double ¼-in (5-mm) hem and press then pin them.

With the feed dogs up, set the sewing machine to a medium straight stitch and sew the hems, close to the folded-over edge. Measure the diameter of the buttons. On one of the back pieces, make two evenly-spaced buttonholes (see page 130).

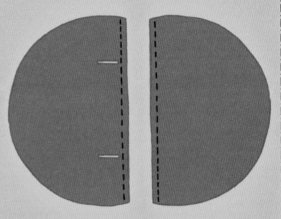

4 Iron the main fabric front piece so it's nice and flat. Then, using all the bits of fabric you cut out and the motifs you have made, compose your design. Collage the flowers, dots, spots, birds, circles, and butterflies so that they sweep and twist and twirl around each other: overlap, layer up, and play with the design, and have lots of fun!

When you've found the perfect composition, lightly glue each piece in place with a dab of fabric glue. Then get lots of different coloured threads and free-machine embroider (see page 130) around all the elements. Add stitching detail to the butterflies and birds, and stitch around the edges of all the flowers. Sew swirls and curls in different colours—and if your machine has different embroidery stitches, try those out, too.

When you're happy with the embroidery, add beads, sequins, and buttons. This project should be a wonderful whirl of colors and fabrics and stitches and sparkles.

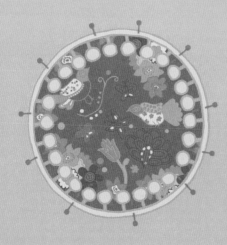

5 Pin the bobble trim around the edge of the cushion front, so that the bobbles are facing inward, as shown.

6 Right side up, lay the embroidered front piece flat. Right side down, lay the back piece with buttonholes on top of the front piece, matching the raw edges so that the buttonholes are more or less in the middle. Lay the other back piece right side down on top of this, with the hem overlapping the buttonholes. Taking a ½-in (1-cm) seam allowance, machine sew around the perimeter.

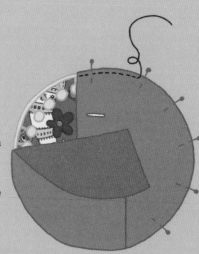

7 Turn the cover right sides out and mark where the buttons should be. Sew on the buttons, then pop in the pillow form (cushion pad).

Plump up your finished masterpiece and marvel at your wizardry. No cats allowed.

Decorations

Beautifully bejeweled bird hanging

This playful bird hanging is a lovely project for both children and grown-ups to make. A perfect decoration for homes and offices, and really fun to do!

Template on page 142

Crafty needs!

Template on page 142

Scraps of fabrics of your choice

Fading fabric marker

Pins, needles, and scissors

Embroidery flosses (threads) in colors of your choice

Buttons

Sewing machine

Sewing threads to match fabrics

Toy stuffing

Ribbon

Thick embroidery floss (thread)

Beads of different sizes and colors

Bell

1 Enlarge the template by 200 percent and draw onto fabric two bodies and two wings for each bird needed. (Look through your pieces of fabrics and try to use different ones for the body and the wings of each bird.) Cut out all the shapes.

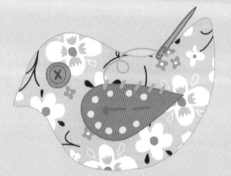

2 Using embroidery floss (thread) and straight stitch (see page 132), sew a wing to the right side of each of the bird body pieces. You can embellish the wings with buttons or beads for added decoration. Sew on buttons to give your bird eyes.

3 Pin two body pieces right sides together. Set the sewing machine to a medium straight stitch (see page 128) and, taking a ½-in (1-cm) seam allowance, sew around the bird, leaving a gap for turning through. Turn the bird right side out. Stuff it so it is nice and plump, then slip stitch (see page 132) the gap closed.

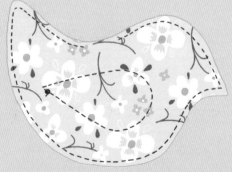

4 To add a tail, loop a piece of ribbon three times and sew it onto the tail end of the bird. Sew on a button over the ends of the loops.

5 Thread a needle with a long length of thick embroidery floss (thread) and tie a bell to the end. Thread on beads to make a 4-in (10-cm) string of beads. Now you can add the first bird. Push the needle through the center bottom of the bird and out through the top. Thread on another 4in (10cm) of beads. Continue this process until you have added all the birds to the hanging. When you have added the last bird, thread on a final 4in (10cm) of beads and tie a small knot immediately above the last bead. To hang the birds, make a large loop in the floss (thread), knotting it just above the last bead.

Stylish scraps bunting

Friends are coming for a barbecue, but you've got no food and the grill hasn't been cleaned for a year. NEVER FEAR! You have super-stylish bunting to glamorize the garden! Everybody will admire it so much they'll forget about the absence of lunch!

1 Cut out triangles for as many pennants as will fit along the length of the bias binding, cutting two triangles for every pennant. (If you want an even quicker way to make the bunting, you can buy kits with the fabric already cut for you. I used a My Poppet one here as their fabrics are gorgeous, see page 133 for details.) Space the pennants evenly and remember to leave a bit of binding free at each end to hang up the bunting with. You can make the triangles whatever size you like; mine are 7½in (19cm) from top to tip and the same across the top. Organize the triangles into good-looking pairs.

2 Pin each pair of triangles right sides together. Set the sewing machine to a medium straight stitch (see page 128) and, taking a ¼-in (5-mm) seam allowance, sew the two sloping sides. Trim the tip of the pennant in the same way you clip a corner (see page 130). Turn it right side out and press. Make sure the tip is pushed out so that the pennant is as triangular as possible.

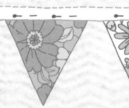

3 Press the bias binding in half lengthwise. Pin pennants into the fold, making sure they're evenly spaced.

Crafty needs!

Bias binding the length you want the bunting to be, allowing a bit at each end for ties

Lots of scraps of fabric

Iron

Pins, needles, and scissors

Sewing machine

Sewing thread to match binding

4 Zigzag stitch or straight stitch along the length of the bias tape, sewing all the pennants in place and removing the pins as you go.

Hang the bunting in the garden or in your home for an instant ray of sunshine.

Fabric appliqué illustration "Walkies"

One of my favorite things to do is appliqué illustration. You can get creative and use your imagination to its fullest, and your own unique style can really shine through. Here is a simple example, but once you've practiced stitching and you feel more confident, your designs can become more adventurous.

Crafty needs!

Fabrics

Iron

Template on page 142

Fusible webbing (optional)

Fading fabric marker

Pins, needles, and scissors

Fabric glue (optional)

Sewing machine with embroidery foot

Sewing threads in colors of your choice

Embroidery floss (thread)

Frame or canvas

Heavy-duty stapler if stretching over a canvas

1 Choose a background fabric, which should measure about 17 x 13in (43 x 33cm) for this design, and fabrics for the appliqué. Iron them all so they're nice and crisp. Enlarge the template by 200 percent and cut out all the separate elements. If you are using fusible webbing (see page 128), draw around the elements onto the paper backing and iron the webbing onto the wrong side of the appropriate bits of fabric. Otherwise, draw around the elements straight onto the fabrics and cut out the shapes.

2 Take the fabric you've chosen for the grass and press under a ½-in (1-cm) hem along the top. Position it onto the background fabric and pin or glue it (see page 128) in place. Use a decorative machine stitch to sew along the top of the grass, then straight stitch (see page 128) around the other edges to hold them in place (you won't see these edges).

3 Collage all the appliqué elements onto the background fabric and pin or glue them in place. Then free-machine embroider (see page 130) around all the pieces with a straight stitch. "Color in" her shoes by going back and forth, and use different-colored threads for the lion's collar and the lady's lips. More detailed areas, such as the faces, may take a bit of practice: if you find them a bit tricky with a sewing machine, use a needle and thread to hand-embroider features instead.

4 Then using black embroidery floss (thread), or whichever color you prefer, chain stitch (see page 132) a lead from the lady to the lion's collar. Give your picture a final iron, then choose a frame to put it in: you'll notice the difference once it's presented in this way. If you decide to stretch the appliqué over a canvas, staple the ends of the fabric alternately to avoid it pulling and distorting the image.

Hang the illustration on a wall and marvel at your creative flair, then experiment with your own designs. To the left is an example of one of my own favorite canvases.

Marvelously individual appliqué portrait

Here's a quirky and creative alternative to a hanging a photo on a wall. It's really not difficult to use fabric and stitch to create an instantly inspiring, and unique, piece of art.

Crafty needs!

A photo of the person

A scanner and printer or photocopier

Canvas to stretch the portrait over

Tracing paper

Pencil

Pins, needles, and scissors

Fading fabric marker

Fabrics for background and appliqué design

Interfacing (optional)

Iron

Fabric glue (optional)

Sewing machine with embroidery foot

Sewing threads in colors of your choice

Buttons (optional)

Heavy-duty stapler

1 When you've chosen the photo you'd like to use, either scan and print it or photocopy it, enlarging it to fit your canvas. If you've chosen a very large canvas, you will have to print out tiled sections of the image, piece them together like a jigsaw, then tape them together. Now lay the tracing paper over the image and draw over the areas of the face and/or body you'd like to include in your final piece. It's best to pick out specific features and keep it as simple as possible. You may need to use several pieces of tracing paper for different areas.

2 Cut out all the areas you've drawn around and choose the fabrics you'd like to use for them in the design. Then use your cut-out pieces of tracing paper as templates to draw around each section and cut it out. You may find it easier to pin the tracing paper to the fabric and cut around each piece.

3 Choose a fabric for the background—it needs to be at least 5in (13cm) bigger than the canvas on each side. Iron the fabric so that it's flat and crisp, then lay the canvas on top of it. On the fabric, mark the edges of the canvas with pins so that you know where to place your appliqué, then put the canvas to one side.

4 Collage all your cut-out pieces onto the background until you have the composition you want, then pin or glue (see page 128) them in place. Iron interfacing (see page 128) to the back of the background fabric if you want to give it extra strength. On the sewing machine, free-machine embroider (see page 130) the design to add details and define the outlines. "Draw" around the eyes, eyebrows, mouth, and creases in clothing with your needle; "color in" areas like eyebrows or eyes with different-colored threads. Go over your stitching several times to give a sketchy, scribbled look to the design. You can also hand-sew embellishments such as buttons to the design, if that works for you.

5 When you're happy with the appliqué, remove the pins and iron out any puckers in the fabric. Place the fabric on the front of the canvas, making sure the design looks straight and well positioned. Pull the fabric taut and staple it to the back of the wooden frame, stapling from the middle outward on each edge, and putting in a few staples at a time on each edge to avoid the fabric wrinkling.

Hang your picture on a wall and admire! This project is perfect for gifts, and the design possibilities are endless. The technique works brilliantly with pets, too.

Lavender hearts

Lavender is thought to have some health benefits, including helping us to sleep and to fight off colds, and it just smells so lovely. So these lavender-filled hearts are good for hanging around the home as decorations, or for giving as gifts

Crafty needs!

Template on page 142

Fabric for hearts

Fading fabric marker

Pins, needles, and scissors

Sewing machine

Sewing thread to match fabric

Iron

Soft polyester stuffing

Dried lavender

8-in (20-cm) length of ribbon

2 buttons per heart

1 Enlarge the template by 200 percent and cut out two heart shapes from fabric. Pin them right sides together. Set the sewing machine to a small straight stitch (see page 128) and, taking a ½-in (1-cm) seam allowance, sew around the edge of the heart, starting on one side and leaving a ¾-in (2cm) gap for turning through. Then snip notches out of the seam allowance around the curves of the heart (see page 130) and trim the point at the bottom to avoid puckering. Turn the heart right side out and press.

2 Lightly fill the heart with soft polyester stuffing, and then top up with a handful of lavender until it's nice and plump. Then slip stitch the opening closed.

3 Fold one end of the ribbon over the other so that you have a loop and the two ends hang down. Position the crossover on the V at the top of the heart, and hand-sew it in place with a couple of stitches; try to use a thread that blends nicely with the fabric you've chosen.

4 Then choose two buttons, position one on the crossover and one on the back of the heart. Stitch in place, stitching through the ribbon and the heart. The buttons will make the heart indent slightly where they are sewn and give it a nice, curved 3-D shape.

You've finished! Hang your heart in your bedroom or at a window and let the lovely lavender fragrance fill the room.

Funky fabric flowers

Here's an easy-peasey but oh-so-effective project for you to try—and another perfect way to use up all those scraps of fabric you have lying around.

1 Choose a selection of fabrics for the petals. It's fun to play around with different designs and mix-and-match until you have a combination that works well. Alternatively, you could use matching or toning fabrics for each flower if you wanted. Using compasses, draw on paper a circle with a 3-in (8-cm) radius and cut it out to make a template. Cut out five fabric circles for one flower and press them so they are nice and crisp.

Crafty needs!

5 small pieces of fabric

Paper

Compasses

Fading fabric marker

Pins, needles, and scissors

Iron

Strong sewing thread to tone with fabrics

Button

Glue gun or strong fabric glue

Florist's tape or green ribbon

Florist's wire

Scrap of felt

2 Fold a circle in half so it's a semi-circle, press it, fold it in half again so it's the shape of a slice of pizza, and press it again. Repeat with each circle of fabric. Then starting at one end of the curved edge, and leaving a 4-in (10-cm) tail of thread, sew a line of running stitch (see page 132) around the curved edge.

3 Now pull the loose ends of the threads until the fabric petal is gathered up. Then, without cutting the thread, sew a line of running stitch along the curved edge of the next petal so that the two petals are strung onto the same piece of thread. Pull up the gathers, pushing the second petal along the thread to sit tightly against the first one.

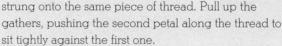

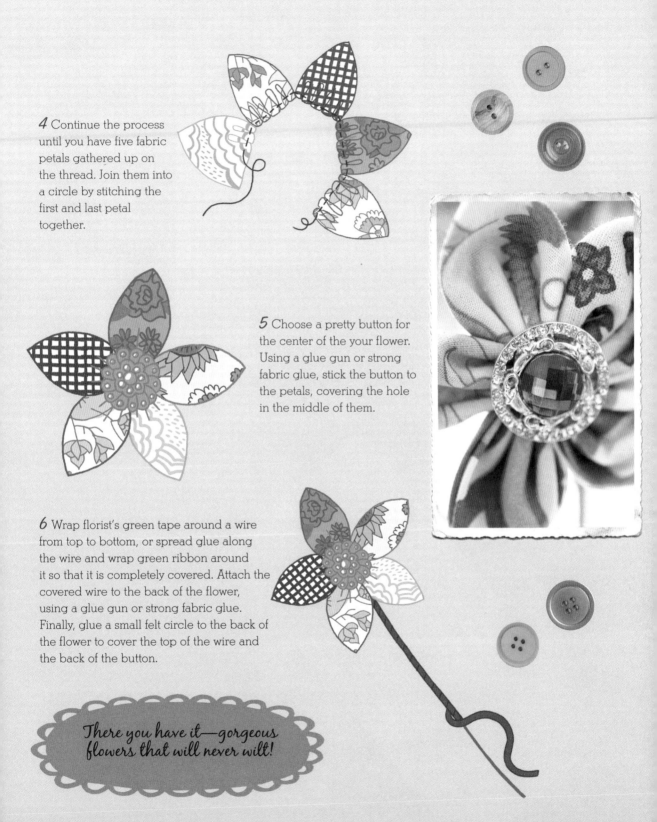

4 Continue the process until you have five fabric petals gathered up on the thread. Join them into a circle by stitching the first and last petal together.

5 Choose a pretty button for the center of the your flower. Using a glue gun or strong fabric glue, stick the button to the petals, covering the hole in the middle of them.

6 Wrap florist's green tape around a wire from top to bottom, or spread glue along the wire and wrap green ribbon around it so that it is completely covered. Attach the covered wire to the back of the flower, using a glue gun or strong fabric glue. Finally, glue a small felt circle to the back of the flower to cover the top of the wire and the back of the button.

There you have it—gorgeous flowers that will never wilt!

Cool customized lampshade

Transform an old or boring lampshade into a seriously splendid interior accessory with this fun and fulfilling project.

1 You'll need to make a template from your lampshade in order to cut out the fabric. To do this, tie some string or yarn securely around the lampshade from top to bottom; this will be your starting point.

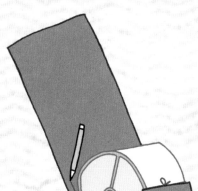

2 Next, lay a big piece of paper, (newspaper or brown parcel paper work well) flat and place the lampshade on top, with the wrapped string against one end. Carefully roll the lampshade across the paper, marking the edges of the shade with the pencil as you go. Stop once your lampshade has rolled back to its starting point (where you tied the string). Add 1in (2.5cm) to the top and bottom edges and one short end of the template. Use this as a template to cut out the lampshade fabric.

3 From favorite fabrics cut out flowers, butterflies, or paisley patterns you like. Use the butterfly from the mobile project (see page 56) and the bird from the tea towel project (see page 14), enlarging them to suit. Cut them out of fabrics,

making best use of patterns for the breasts, wings, and tails. Use tracing paper as a guide, or just cut by eye—I find the latter will often give creative results. On the background fabric, use the fabric marker to draw swirls for the branches the birds sit on. Place all the pieces on the fabric, layering up flowers and swirls and butterflies. Keep all the decoration at least 1in (2.5cm) in from the edges of the fabric. Lightly glue everything in place (see page 128).

Crafty needs!

Round lampshade or lampshade frame

String or yarn

Large piece of paper

Pencil

Tape measure

Fabrics, a big piece to cover the lampshade and a collection of small pieces for the appliqué design

Templates on page 134 and 140

Pins, needles, and scissors

Fading fabric marker

Fabric glue or spray adhesive

Buttons, sequins, or embellishments (optional)

Sewing machine

Sewing threads in colors of your choice

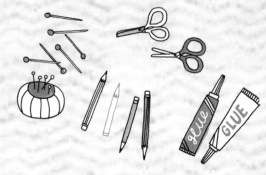

The thicker the background fabric, the less the light will shine through, and if you choose a colored fabric, then the light will be slightly tinted when the lamp is switched on. I've chosen a very thin white fabric with a tint of green.

4 When the glue is dry, take the length of fabric to your sewing machine and free-machine embroider (see page 130) around the elements of the design. Try out different embroidery stitches if your machine has them—if not, you can add some by hand (see page 132). Sew swirls and scribbles and wiggles and different shapes, and add details to the birds and butterflies. Then hand-sew on buttons for the birds' eyes and the flower centers, and add sequins and beads if you fancy.

5 When you're happy with the appliqué, carefully press under a ½-in (1-cm) hem along the top and bottom edges and one short edge. Then, spray a little adhesive or spread a little glue along the vertical seam on the lampshade and stick the raw short edge of the fabric to it, making sure the edge is in line with the seam. Smooth the fabric so that it's nice and flat, then wrap it around the lampshade a short section at a time, sticking it down as you go. Fold the top and bottom edges of the fabric over the edges of the lampshade and glue them down, making sure there are no puckers in the fabric and that it's wrapped neatly and evenly.

Techniques

The techniques used in this book are nice and simple, though if you haven't come across a particular one before, practice on some scrap fabric before you start your project.

Preparing fabric

If you are recycling fabric from old clothes or soft furnishings, launder it to make sure it's nice and fresh. You can cut around permanent stains, but if the item is a bit smelly, then your project will smell, too!

If you are using multiple fabrics and the finished project will need laundering at some point in its life, then do make sure that the fabrics you're using can be washed together and that colors won't run. You can test for color-fastness by dipping a bit of the fabric in warm water and then squeezing it with white kitchen paper.

If the fabric is creased, give it a quick press before you use it; it's always easier to work on smooth, crisp fabric.

Using templates

All the templates you'll need are on pages 134–143, and each project tells you how much to enlarge the template by on a photocopier. Sometimes you'll need to flip a template to produce a front and back; the projects will tell you when to do this. For outlines, just cut out the template and draw around it with a fading fabric marker. To transfer details within the template onto fabric, you can tape the template to a window with masking tape, then tape the fabric over it. You should be able to trace off the detail onto the fabric. But do feel free to draw your own details, just using the template as reference.

Attaching motifs before sewing

If the motifs are quite big, you can pin them onto the background fabric before sewing them in place. However, if there are lots of small pieces, it will be easiest to glue them on. Use proper fabric glue and just little dabs of it in the middle of each piece; try not to use lots of glue or it'll stain the fabric and make it gloopy and difficult to sew. Alternatively, you can baste (tack) pieces in place with hand stitches in a contrast color thread (to make them easy to see and take out later).

You can also use fusible webbing to hold pieces in place. This is a heat-sensitive film on a paper backing that you iron onto the wrong side of the fabric. You then draw the shape you want on the paper backing, cut it out, peel the backing off, and iron the shape onto the background. You can buy a special sew-able webbing that won't clog up your machine needle as much. Always follow the manufacturer's instructions when using fusible webbing to avoid mistakes.

Fusible interfacing

This is interfacing with a heat-sensitive film on one side. If you are using thin fabric, you just iron it onto the wrong side of your fabric to stiffen and strengthen it. It's always a good idea to test a bit of interfacing on a scrap of the fabric first, as it can pucker permanently.

Using a sewing machine

You don't need to be very skilled with a sewing machine to make projects in this book, but if you've not used one very often, or it's a while since you last stitched, then spend some time polishing up on your skills by sewing bits of scrap fabric to get used to it. As well as ordinary straight stitching, there is a lot of free-machine embroidery in many of the projects (see page 130), so you will need an embroidery/darning foot for your sewing machine if you haven't got one. Other than that, you only need a straight foot and a zigzag foot.

It's always a good idea to read the sewing machine instruction manual again to make sure you're threading and using the machine properly.

The stitch you'll use most will be a medium-length straight stitch, so test that out. Also experiment with any zigzag and decorative stitches your machine might have and, if appropriate, make a note of the machine settings that work best with each one.

The most important thing to get right is the tension. There'll be a dial on the front of your machine that you turn to adjust the spool tension; the larger the number, the tighter the tension.

Here, the top tension is too loose and the top thread is being pulled through to the bobbin side of the seam.

Here, the top tension is too tight and the bobbin thread is being pulled to the top.

This diagram shows balanced tension, with the top and bobbin threads interlocking within the layers of fabric.

Before you start each project, sew a seam on a scrap bit of the project fabric to check that your tension is right.

On the throat plate (the metal plate under the needle) of the machine, there will be marks showing different widths of seam allowance. Just pick the width you need and line up the raw edge of the fabric with the mark. Sew quite slowly, keeping the edge of the fabric on the mark, and your seam or hem will be neat and accurate.

Topstitching

I use this technique in some projects and if you've not done it before it's definitely one you should practice. You sew a line of straight stitch very close to the edge of the project; about ⅛in (2mm) in from the edge is good. The trick is to position the fabric under the needle and lower the needle into the fabric to check it'll be sewing in the right place. Then, if there isn't a mark on the throat plate in the right place, stick a piece of masking tape to the plate at the edge of the fabric. Keep the edge of the fabric against the tape as you sew and your topstitching will look great.

Free-machine embroidery

I think this is the nicest way of using a sewing machine. "Draw" details onto the project with the needle and "color in" areas. Go over stitching several times to give a sketchy, scribbled look; it doesn't have to be neat to look great. This is another technique you'll want to practice if you're not familiar with it. The best thing to do is to experiment on a piece of scrap fabric until you feel confident; this gives you the opportunity to adjust the tension, too.

Your sewing machine will have feed dogs that come up into the throat plate as you sew and pull the fabric through. To embroider you need to drop the feed dogs; your sewing machine manual will tell you how to do it on your particular machine. Once the dogs are down you can move the fabric in any direction under the needle, as fast or as slow as you wish.

You'll need a free-machine embroidery foot, sometimes called a darning foot or a free-motion foot. This stops the fabric from lifting while you sew. You might find it helpful to fit the fabric into an embroidery hoop while you sew, to keep it flat and taut and prevent any puckering. You can buy special easy-to-use hoops for machine embroidery, or use a traditional wooden one—it'll work just as well.

Once you're ready, set the stitch length on the machine to zero, and off you go. Start slowly to get the feel of the stitching and see how fast you need to move the fabric to achieve the look you want. Think of the fabric as a piece of paper and the needle as a pencil and reverse it in your brain so you're moving the paper to make the design. Be VERY careful to keep your fingers away from the needle as you move the fabric about under it.

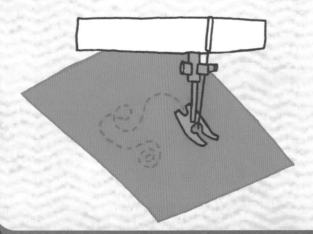

Trimming corners

If you've seamed a corner, you need to clip off excess fabric before you turn the project right side out to ensure that the finished corner is neat and square. Cut off the fabric across the corner as shown, cutting about ⅛in (2mm) away from the line of stitching.

Notching curves

Curved seams need notches cutting out of the seam allowances so that, when the project is turned right side out, the seam allowances lie flat and the seam isn't puckered. Cut small notches with the tips of the scissors to about ⅛in (2mm) away from the line of stitching. Space the notches about ¾in (2cm) apart on the curves.

Making buttonholes

If you have an automatic buttonhole feature on your sewing machine, use that and a buttonhole foot to sew the buttonholes. To sew buttonholes manually, set your machine to a narrow zigzag. Sew down the left side of the marked buttonhole. Lift the presser foot and pivot the fabric 180 degrees. Lower the presser foot and double the stitch width. Hold the fabric firmly, so that it doesn't slip, and let the machine make a few side-to-side stitches. Return the stitch width to its prior setting and sew up the other side of the buttonhole, then make a few longer stitches, as before. Using your seam unpicker, cut through the fabric to open the buttonholes, being careful not to cut the threads.

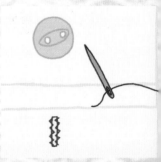

Making a pom-poms
These are quite addictive to make—be warned!

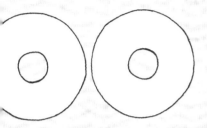

1 Cut out two circles of card the size you want the pom-pom to be. Cut a smaller circle out of the middle of each, so they look like rings.

2 Place the rings on top of each other and, using manageable lengths, wind knitting yarn around the rings, using an embroidery needle if it makes it easier. Feed the yarn through the circle in the middle and wind it around the card. If you come to the end of a length of yarn, there's no need to tie the ends; just make sure that the end is on the outside of the ring rather than the inside. Continue this until all the card is covered and the hole is nearly full of wound yarn.

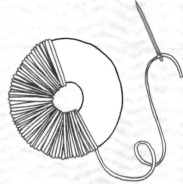

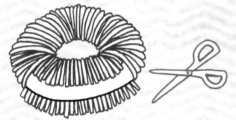

3 Now cut the yarn around the outside of the rings, a little bit at a time.

4 Thread another piece of yarn between the card rings and tie it tightly—very tightly—around the bunched strands of yarn.

5 Remove the cardboard rings—you might need to cut them off. Trim any unruly ends of yarn.

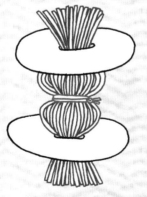

Backstitch

Bring the needle through the fabric and take a short backward stitch on the stitching line. Bring the needle through a stitch-length in front of the first stitch. Take the needle down where it first came through and repeat to sew the seam.

Blanket stitch

From the front, make a stitch through the fabric, coming out on the stitching line. Loop the working thread under the point of the needle. Pull the needle through and tighten the stitch. Continue in this way, spacing the stitches evenly for a neat finish.

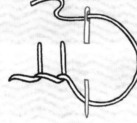

To avoid distorting stitches or puckering fabric, tighten the thread gently.

Chain stitch

Bring the needle through the fabric at the start of the stitching line. Take the needle back down right beside where it came up and bring it through again at the end of the first stitch.

Loop the working thread under the point of the needle and pull the needle and thread through to make a neat loop. Take the needle down right beside where it came up in the loop and bring it up at the end of the next stitch. Continue in this way to create a chain of loops. Anchor the last loop with a small straight stitch over the end of it.

Running stitch

Make a series of small stitches along the stitching line. They can be of even lengths and equally spaced, or more random, whichever you prefer the look of.

Satin stitch

Make a small straight stitch across the area to be covered. Work a second stitch right next to the first one. Continue in this way, butting the stitches as closely as possible, until the area is filled with stitching.

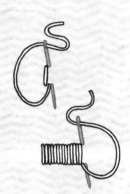

Some sewing machines have a satin stitch setting, or you can experiment with a very tight zigzag stitch.

Slip stitch

This is used to close gaps in seams. Bring the needle up through one piece of fabric at the start of the gap. Take it across to the other piece and make a tiny stitch through that. Pull the stitch tight, but not

so tight that the fabric puckers. Take the needle across to the other piece and make the next tiny stitch. Continue in this way to sew up the whole gap.

Straight stitch

Make a small straight stitch where needed. Repeat as required!

Crafty Supplies

To be a crafty stitcher, there are some essential things that you will need...

- Sewing machine
- A free-machine embroidery foot (for appliqué designs and "drawing" with thread)
- Good-quality threads in a nice range of colors
- Pins and needles (and for somewhere to keep them safe, make your own pins and needles case—see page 64)
- Fabric scissors (paper scissors just don't cut it! S'cuse the pun)
- A magic fading fabric pen (pencils can be used, but they're not magical)
- Iron and ironing board or mat
- Measuring tape
- Unpicker (for crafty mistakes)

Here are the websites for my favorite fabric suppliers.

www.amybutlerdesign.com
www.michaelmillerfabrics.com
www.heatherbaileydesign.com
www.aliceapple.co.uk
www.liberty.co.uk
stores.ebay.co.uk/Pixie-Rose-Crafts
www.thefeltfairy.com
www.freespiritfabric.com
www.mypoppet.com.au

US Suppliers

Hobby Lobby
www.hobbylobby.com

Michaels
www.michaels.com

Joann Fabric & Craft Stores
www.joann.com

UK Suppliers

VV Rouleaux
www.vvrouleaux.com

John Lewis
www.johnlewis.com

Hobbycraft
www.hobbycraft.co.uk

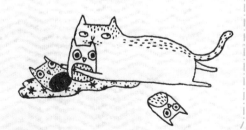

Templates

Keep clean and stay cool apron, page 10.
Enlarge templates by 200%.

Bird's throat

Bird's back

Bird's tummy

Whole bird

Tantalizing tea towel, page 14.
Enlarge templates by 200%.

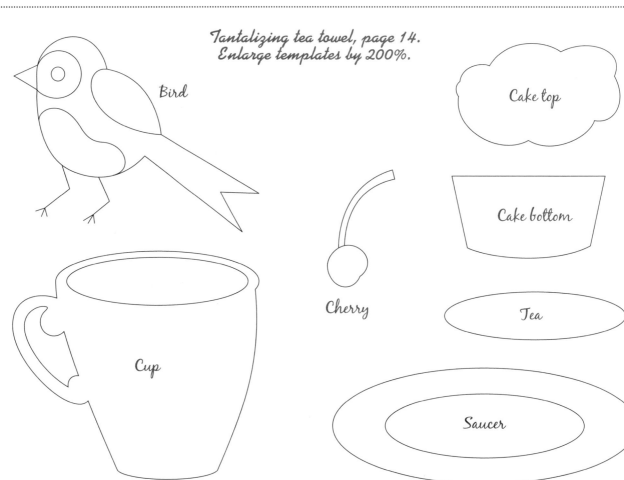

Bird

Cake top

Cake bottom

Cherry

Tea

Cup

Saucer

Umbrella

Hand

Face

Hair

Coat

Skirt

Complete
design

Left leg

Right leg

Left sock

Right sock

Left shoe

Right shoe

The fly-away-umbrella tea cozy, page 17.
Enlarge templates by 200%.

Pretty-pleasing-sugar-on-top placemats, page 20.
Enlarge template by 300%. Template shows half the design.

Woodland critters table runner, page 22.
Enlarge templates by 200%.

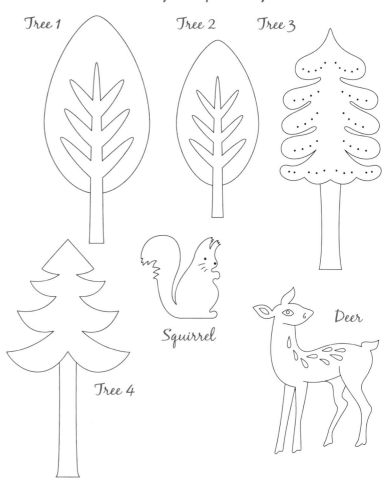

Tree 1

Tree 2

Tree 3

Tree 4

Squirrel

Deer

Hop, skip, and a pair of oven mitts, page 25.
Enlarge apple template by 200% and mitt template by 400%.

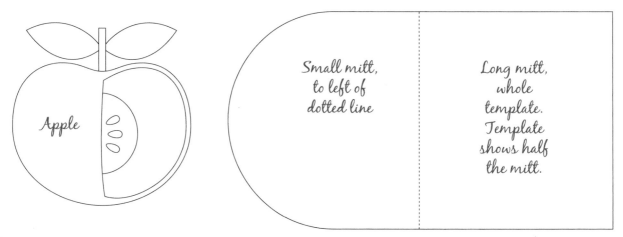

Apple

Small mitt, to left of dotted line

Long mitt, whole template. Template shows half the mitt.

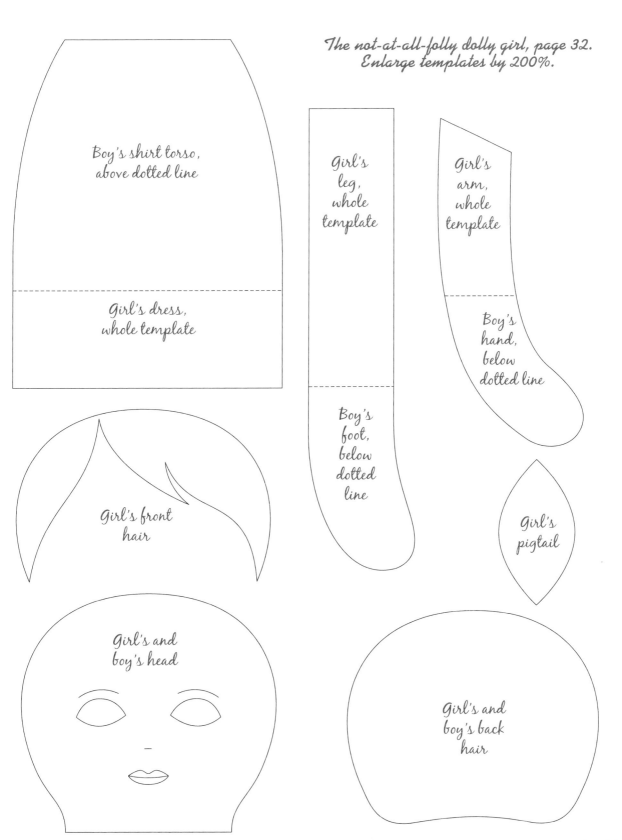

The not-at-all-folly dolly girl, page 32.
Enlarge templates by 200%.

Boy's shirt torso,
above dotted line

Girl's dress,
whole template

Girl's
leg,
whole
template

Girl's
arm,
whole
template

Boy's
hand,
below
dotted line

Boy's
foot,
below
dotted
line

Girl's front
hair

Girl's
pigtail

Girl's and
boy's head

Girl's and
boy's back
hair

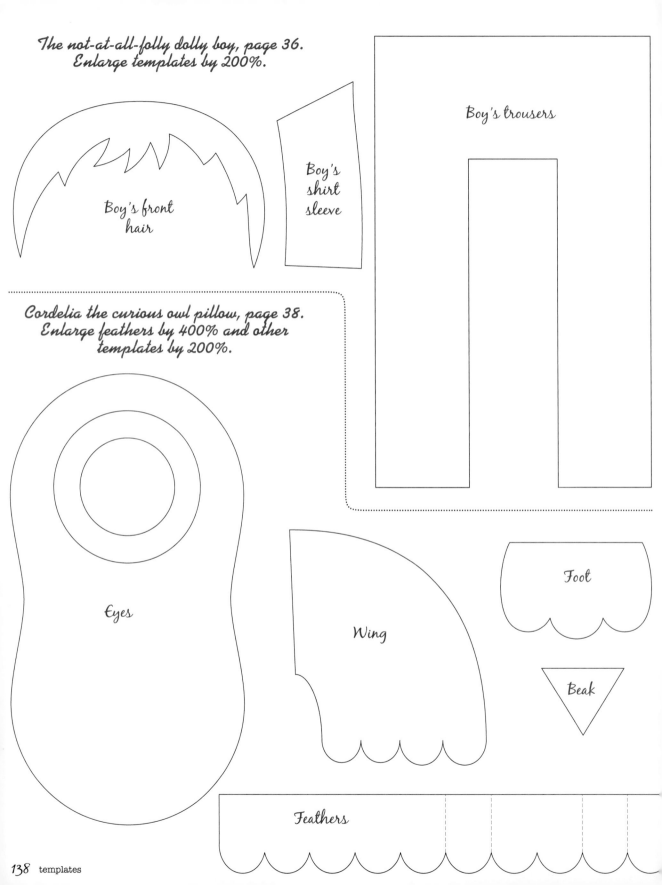

The not-at-all-folly dolly boy, page 36.
Enlarge templates by 200%.

Boy's front hair

Boy's shirt sleeve

Boy's trousers

Cordelia the curious owl pillow, page 38.
Enlarge feathers by 400% and other templates by 200%.

Eyes

Wing

Foot

Beak

Feathers

Bonkers bobtail bunnies, page 42.
Enlarge template by 400%.

George the giraffe, page 44.
Enlarge body template by 600%
and other templates by 400%.

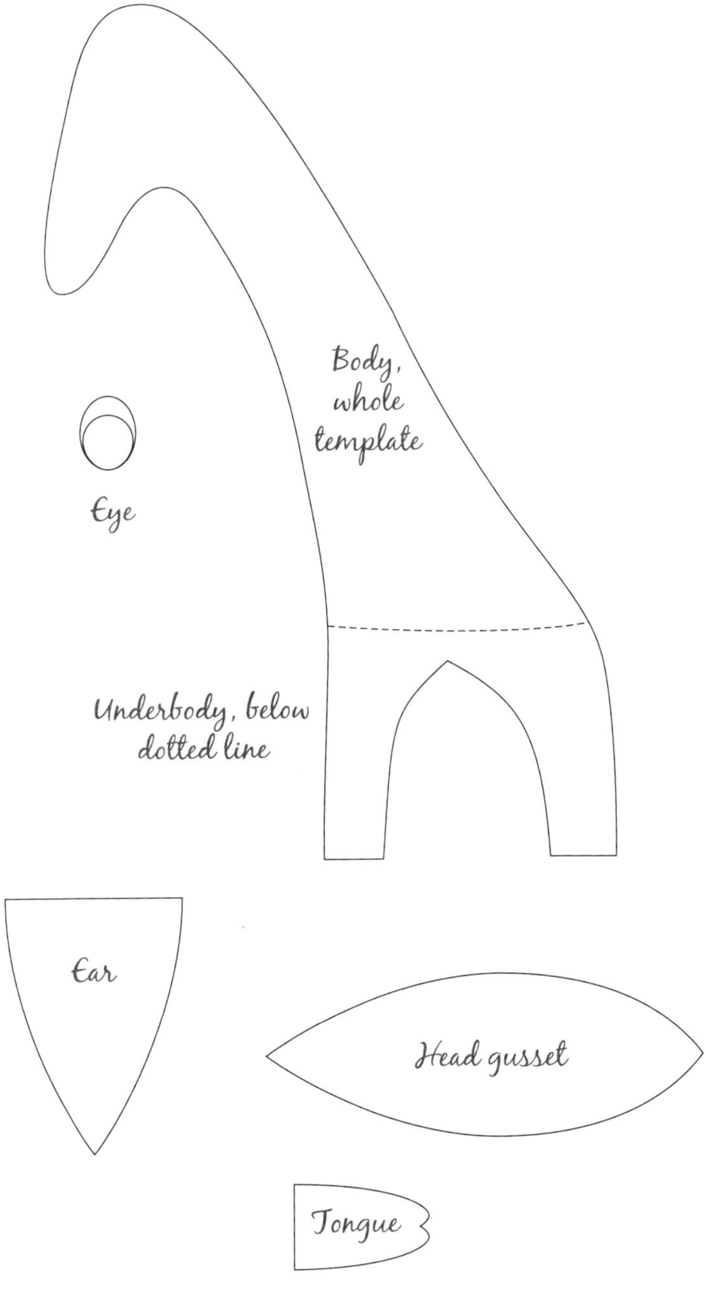

Body,
whole
template

Eye

Underbody, below
dotted line

Ear

Head gusset

Tongue

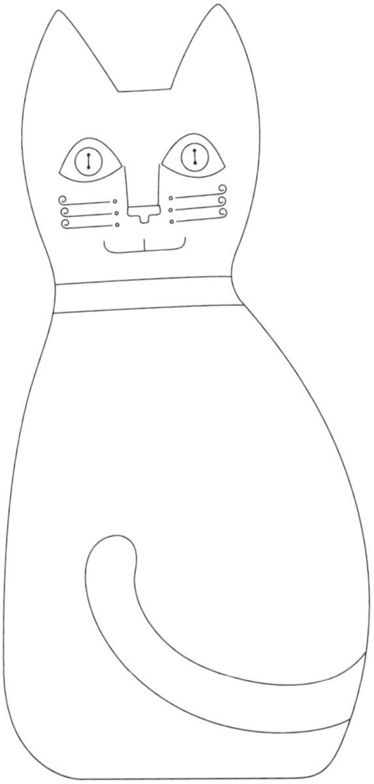

Cute-as-a-kitten doorstop, page 48.
Enlarge template by 400%.

Beautiful baby bib, page 54.
Enlarge template by 400%.

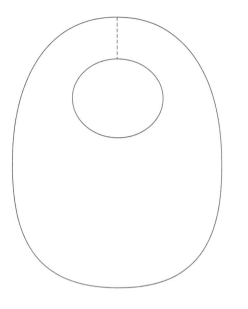

Springtime showers mobile, page 56.
Enlarge templates by 200%.

Large and small flowers and
flower circle

Butterfly

Cloud

Raindrops and rainbows
mini quilt, page 60.
Enlarge templates by 200%.

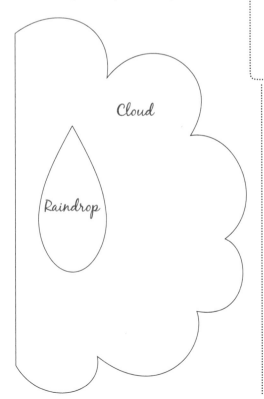

Cloud

Raindrop

Pins and needle case,
page 64.
Enlarge templates
by 200%.

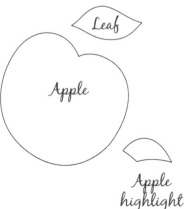

Leaf

Apple

Apple
highlight

Snazzy coat hanger
cover, page 70.
Enlarge templates
by 200%.

Large and
small flowers

Pillowcase tote bag, page 74.
Enlarge templates by 200%.

Butterfly

Sleepy head pillow,
page 88.
Enlarge templates
by 200%.

Cat

Breakfast at Tiffany's eye mask,
page 92.
Enlarge templates
by 200%.

Eyelid
and
lashes

Mask

Butterfly

Head

Hair

Hands

Right body

Left body

Dress

Complete
girl

Butterfly catcher pillow, page 96.
Enlarge templates by 200%.

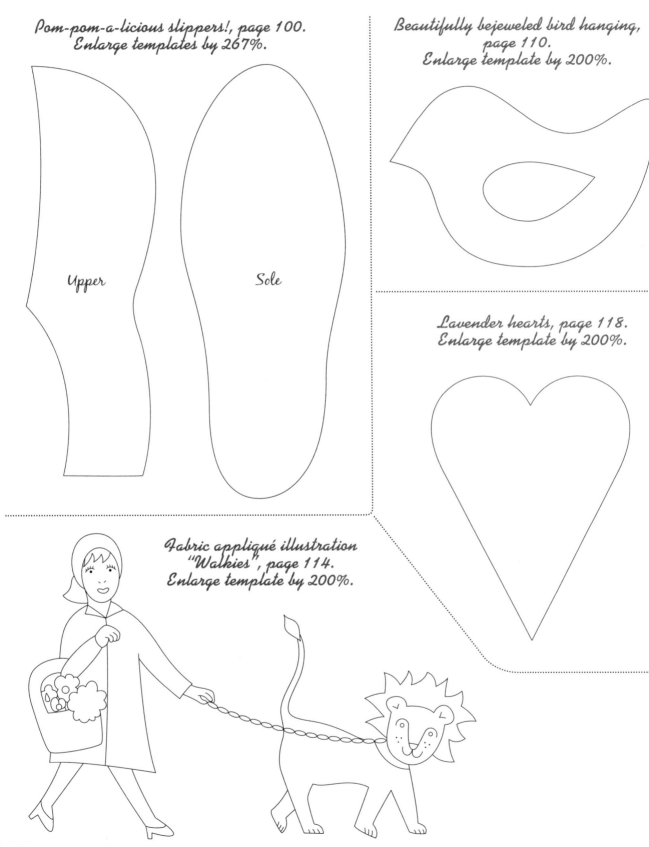

Pom-pom-a-licious slippers!, page 100.
Enlarge templates by 267%.

Upper

Sole

Beautifully bejeweled bird hanging,
page 110.
Enlarge template by 200%.

Lavender hearts, page 118.
Enlarge template by 200%.

Fabric appliqué illustration
"Walkies", page 114.
Enlarge template by 200%.

Index

Acknowledgments

I'd like to thank my lovely helpers sent from heaven, Kate and Jenny; thank you for all your hard work and help keeping everything in control while I was making this book.

My mum for letting me take over her spare room (and home) as my studio and making a huge mess.

A special thank you to my brother Christian for lots of hard-working sleepless nights, cups of tea, and amazing design skills.

Huge big special thank you to Amy Butler (www.amybutlerdesign.com), Alice Burrows from Alice Apple (www.aliceapple.co.uk), Heather Bailey (www.heatherbaileydesign.com), and Michael Miller (www.michaelmillerfabrics.com) for donating their beautiful fabrics and so inspiring me to make lovely things.

Cindy, Sally, Pete, Kate, and Claire at Cico for all your niceness and putting up with my demands and giving me such creative freedom throughout.

Gigantic thanks to Gemma Correll for her amazing talent and adding an extra-special something to my book.

Pippa, Catherine, and Charlie for advice and helping hands.

Thank you to my best friend Jake, who kept me company and made me laugh while I worked, for as long as he could.

And last but definitely not least, D-fran, who has supported and encouraged me and never stopped believing in me. I couldn't have done it without you.